When Sparrows Fall

Valerie Lee

Cover art by
Gary Manly

*Love,
Valerie
Lee*

TEACH Services, Inc.
P U B L I S H I N G
www.TEACHServices.com • (800) 367-1844

Copyright © 2016 TEACH Services, Inc.

ISBN-13: 978-1-4796-0684-9 (Paperback)

ISBN-13: 978-1-4796-0685-6 (ePub)

ISBN-13: 978-1-4796-0686-3 (Mobi)

Library of Congress Control Number: 2016914563

Published by

TEACH Services, Inc.
P U B L I S H I N G
www.TEACHServices.com • (800) 367-1844

To everything there is a season, a time for every purpose under heaven: a time to be born, and a time to die; a time to plant, and a time to pluck what is planted; a time to kill, and a time to heal; a time to break down, and a time to build up; a time to weep, and a time to laugh; a time to mourn, and a time to dance.

(Eccles. 3:1–4)

Table of Contents

PART ONE

A Time for Laughter

"A merry heart does good, like medicine."
(Prov. 17:22)

CHAPTER 1

Back to School

From her third-floor vantage point, Robin Carter observed the back-to-school flurries of activity. She shifted her gaze from the front campus view outside her window and surveyed her small dorm room. Because enrollment was down at the school, Robin was able to score a room to herself. Her mom had helped her decorate a bit before she'd headed home. Robin's twin bed was made with a pretty, flowery bedspread, and she had tacked many photos of friends and family onto the bulletin board behind her desk. Her clothes were all hung neatly in the closet or folded inside the ample drawer space. She had a purple bean bag chair in one corner and a small fridge stocked with milk, yogurt, and juice in another. Her Hot Pot was carefully hidden (they weren't supposed to have them in the dorm, but everyone used them to boil water), and her stash of ramen noodles and mac and cheese was ready to go. Her mom had even left her with lots of other treats: gummy bears, Cool Ranch Doritos, and a big bag of Snickers bites.

She was now a sophomore at Sunnydale Adventist Academy, a Christian boarding secondary school located in Centralia, Missouri. To help keep the students out of trouble, the school was located in the heart of Missouri's rural Amish country—out in the middle of nowhere and surrounded by corn fields. Robin had many happy memories traveling up to this area when she was younger to buy peaches from the local farmers or to enjoy the beautiful scenery. She loved the tranquility of Amish country, whether it was the sight of a horse and buggy trotting down the road or of a covered bridge crossing a peaceful, meandering stream.

Though Robin had been born in Florida, her parents moved to Columbia, Missouri, when she was just a few weeks old, so the Midwest was truly her home. Her brother John completed their family circle one year later, and Robin was often thankful to have a sibling so close in age. *Often* was the key word because when they were getting along, things were great, but when they weren't, their fights were notorious! They were regularly blamed for adding many gray hairs to their parents' heads.

Robin didn't consider herself a big traveler, but the family took trips in the summers to Colorado to go camping and climb mountains, or to Florida to visit her grandfather and her step-grandmother who lived on the beach. She hadn't seen the ocean until she was eleven but still remembered her awe as she stared out at the vast expanse of sea touching the sky at the horizon. She always liked how Missouri was in the middle of the United States, so even though they didn't have a lot of money, with affordable accommodations (campgrounds and her grandpa's house), her family could take these trips with a manageable drive either way.

She had lived in the dorm her freshman year and knew better what to expect this time around. She also wasn't nearly as afraid as she had been a year ago. Since her room faced the front of campus, she was excited about the people-watching entertainment her window would no doubt provide. Her good friend, Hannah, lived next door and several other friends lived just down the hall.

It's going to be a great year, Robin told herself, *especially since Scott remembered me!*

Scott Hayes, a really cute sophomore whom she'd met at the end of last school year, had remembered her at registration and said hi! Scott was tall, with dirty blonde hair and green eyes. He'd moved from California to live with his mom in the spring and attended public school to finish his freshman year. Robin had met him through Richie Snow, her best guy friend. Considering Scott was friends with Richie, it wouldn't be that hard to "bump" into him often.

Scott got even cuter over the summer! She smiled to herself as she turned off the light in her room. She headed to Hannah's room, and the two girls spent the rest of the evening giggling and making predictions about the year ahead.

Beep, beep, beep. It was 5 a.m. and Robin knocked her alarm clock off the desk as she attempted to hit snooze. Robin loved snoozing in the morning and usually set her clock at least a half hour early. Snooze sleep was like stolen sleep. Plus, sometimes she was having a really good dream right before the alarm went off and snoozing allowed her to continue the adventure.

As she retrieved the clock from under her bed, she remembered it was the first day of school and switched on her desk lamp. Breakfast was at six, and she had a 6:50 a.m. class. She certainly wasn't a morning person, but showers always perked her up, so she stumbled out of her room and headed to the bathroom with her shower caddy. Communal showers were one of the disadvantages to living in the dorm. At least they had decent sized stalls, unlike the boys' dorm, which she heard was just one big open shower room. She shuddered at that thought. At fifteen, she was insecure about pretty much everything relating to her body. She'd hit a growth spurt recently, so at least she'd grown out of her chubby and awkward phase, but while her friends were all "blossoming" into visible women, she was still waiting for her turn.

Back in her room, she blow-dried her hair and then turned on her computer to listen to her favorite artist as she figured out what to wear. Before long her mind was lost in the music. Like most girls her age, Robin was into boy bands and other pop artists. David Cook had a voice that was smooth and soothing to hear. He wasn't new to the music scene (his big break was in 2008 when he won his season of American Idol), but she'd discovered him when she and her dad attended a Kansas City Chiefs game during her eighth grade year. When it came time for the national anthem, they announced that the singer was a local, right from Blue Springs, a suburb of Kansas City, and had won American Idol a few years back. Even though she had been so cold by the end of that December game she'd not been able to move her fingers, Robin had loved every minute. It was a special father-daughter outing; now a very fond memory. Perhaps that's why when she returned home, she'd looked up David Cook and ordered every album he sold on Amazon. His music reminded her of those happy moments.

Robin jerked her mind back to the present and stared at her clothes. She didn't consider herself sloppy or anything, but she was a tomboy through and through. She usually threw her shoulder-length light brown hair up into a ponytail and chose clothes for comfort rather than style. It hadn't helped that with the family budget so tight growing up, most of her clothes had been hand-me-downs or had come from the community service center that her maternal grandmother ran. In elementary school, her attire often consisted of sweatpants with a t-shirt or an ugly sweater when it was colder. It still hurt to remember the other kids' teasing remarks or how they'd made such a big deal when she'd worn a new pair of jeans to school and finally matched.

So, despite her history, today she would make an extra effort to look cute. She told herself it was because it was the first day of school, but she knew better. It was for Scott and any other sophomore boys that might talk to her. After finally deciding on a pretty outfit that conformed to the school's dress code of modest business casual, she went back to the bathroom to put on a little makeup. She usually went sans cosmetics, but today she applied a little mascara and some lip gloss. Staring at her reflection in the mirror, she admired the natural highlights the summer sun had given her hair and how the green shirt she'd chosen made her blue-green eyes kind of pop. She liked how her eyes seemed to change color with what she was wearing. Finally satisfied with her appearance, she dropped her toiletries case off in her room, grabbed her backpack, and headed to the cafeteria for breakfast.

She got carried away in conversation with Hannah and lost track of time, so she had to run to the administration (Ad, for short) building when it was time for class. A tardy would get her into trouble and affect her freedom during relaxed study halls. Out of breath and flushed, she made it to Life Skills a minute or two before the bell. She spotted Scott over in the corner with a seat open next to him. Taking a deep breath, she headed over and asked if she could sit beside him.

He grinned, "The spot is all yours."

The desks were arranged in fours, and Robin couldn't believe her good fortune when no one else sat in their section. She had Scott all to herself. She was even more thrilled when he ended up sitting next to her in English and Biology! That night she did a little happy dance when she checked her Facebook and saw a pending friend request from Scott.

This year is shaping up to be my best one yet, she told herself.

The first few days of class flew by. Robin was a dedicated student, so she tried really hard not to be too distracted by Scott's presence, but since he was always whispering jokes and making her laugh, that was very hard to do. She found herself living for the three classes in which they sat together, and considering she didn't have any cooking or other "life" skills and hated grammar, that was a big deal! Again, she couldn't believe her good luck when he agreed to be her Biology lab partner, and she was ecstatic when he signed up to cook bread at their teacher's house on the same day as her for their Life Skills class.

Scott and Richie were both community students, which everyone at Sunnydale called "village," so they didn't live in the dorm. However, they would bring their lunches from home or sometimes buy lunch so that they could eat in the cafeteria with the dorm students. Robin soon found herself eating lunch with Scott and Richie every day. She laughed so hard at their antics that her stomach hurt.

Scott would pretend to feed the hole in his tennis shoe potato chips—he called it "Mr. Adidas shoe"—and would only drink grape soda because it reminded him of his favorite children's medicine. Richie would tell stories about being an upperclassman, like when he scared a freshman girl by hiding his pet hedgehog in a fake anatomy skull and having it jump out at her. Robin remembered the time he did that to her and wondered if his story was about her. Richie was a junior and being closer to graduating gave him an extra level of respect.

Robin had become friends with Richie the year before. She'd been the only freshman in the sophomore PE section. Even though this year she still hadn't completely come out of her shell, last year she had been even more painfully shy. Richie made a point to befriend her and include her in the activities. He'd always picked her to be on his team in basketball and had been there with a high five and a "Good job!" even when she knew she did badly. He'd helped her up when she fell, and he'd even played catch with her, throwing passes with the football and running plays long after his other friends had lost interest.

Richie had the ability to make her laugh no matter how bad her day was, and he had a way of making her feel important. Robin knew he accepted her for who she was and didn't judge her for being awkward and unconfident. She hated the braces on her teeth, especially when her brother called her "Metal Mouth" and her dad told her to stay away from strong magnets. She knew they were trying to be funny, but she was so insecure that it wasn't.

After lunch one day, the two boys tried to teach Robin how to play hacky sack.

"Oops," she grimaced after she kicked it way out of the way for what seemed like the hundredth time.

"It's OK," Richie said, "we weren't good at first either."

"I doubt that," Robin countered. "You two are naturals at everything!"

Scott retrieved the wayward beanbag and kicked it to her with an encouraging, "Try again!"

And that was just who they were. Since Robin was still shy, she didn't know that many people, but Richie and Scott were really friendly and seemed to know everyone. Richie and Scott were good at making her feel comfortable. She knew that they probably did that for everyone else, too. She blushed whenever she thought of Scott's kindness, but she knew he was probably just being friendly and had no romantic interest in her. That didn't stop her from hoping, though.

She kicked the hacky sack back to Scott. It almost made it to him this time. She was getting a little better. Scott passed it to Richie, and the three played until it was time for her and Scott to head to class and Richie to head to work.

All the students worked half the day and had classes half the day. Freshmen and juniors had classes in the morning and worked in the afternoon while sophomores and seniors worked in the morning and had classes in the afternoon. Robin had Life Skills in the morning, but it was before chapel, so it was not part of the split class schedule. She worked for the principal's secretary, Mrs. Hanson, answering the main phone, transferring calls, and doing other miscellaneous office tasks. Scott worked in the cafeteria, and Richie worked at the plastic industry right on campus. There were two factories on campus where students, sixteen and older, could work and earn minimum wage (or more), which was much better than on-campus wages. The downsides were the work was harder and students working at the industries had to work four hours a day instead of three.

"Have fun at work," she called to Richie as she and Scott picked up their backpacks and headed to Bible class.

CHAPTER 2

Fighting Over the Whale

Eying herself again in the mirror, Robin willed herself to leave the women's bathroom and head into the pool area. She hated swimsuits and the way they showed off her body (or lack thereof) and shuddered at the memory of a comment from a mean girl at summer camp comparing her to a board. Fortunately, Robin's mom had helped her pick out a cute new swimsuit for this occasion, and with the addition of her board shorts, she felt she was adequately and modestly covered.

It was the first Saturday night of the year, so the school took all the students into Columbia to celebrate with a pool party. Located about thirty minutes from the school, Columbia was the nearest big town to Sunnydale. Even though Centralia had a community pool, the one in Columbia was bigger and newer, and the students were thrilled to "get away" from campus.

Since Robin's parents lived in the outskirts of Columbia, she had been to this pool many times before and was familiar with how to get into the water as swiftly as possible. Taking a deep breath, she grabbed her beach towel and pushed open the door leading to the pool deck, her flip flops making a comforting noise as she walked. She spotted Hannah in the shallow end and quickly headed into the water towards her.

The water was a little colder than she'd expected, but she knew the best way to acclimate was to dunk herself. Pinching her nose with her fingers, she quickly submersed her whole body. She knew it was juvenile to plug her nose, but she couldn't bring herself not to do it. The water began to "warm up" so she hovered under it, using it to camouflage her body. She looked around for Scott or Richie. Since they were village, they weren't required to come to extracurricular activities, but she really hoped they would decide to come tonight.

Just as she was about to give up hope, her heart did a little flutter as she saw Richie, Scott, and a few other village students strut into the room. She tried not to be too obvious as she admired Scott's shirtless body.

He must work out, she thought.

She watched as Scott went immediately to the diving board and did an impressive...belly flop. As he surfaced, he caught Robin's eye and swam over to where she and Hannah were treading water in the deepest part of the shallow end, allowing them to watch all of the diving board action.

"Hi, Robin! Hi, Hannah!" Scott grinned at the two of them. "Did you see my belly flop?"

Robin nodded at his red chest, "Did you do it on purpose? It looks like it hurt."

"Nah, it only hurts if you hit wrong. And it really gets the blood flowing. You and Hannah should try it!"

"Um, I think I'm..." Robin was interrupted when another sophomore guy came by and purposely splashed them. "Ow!" she yelped wiping at her stinging eyes.

"Are you OK?" Scott was quick to ask. "You aren't wearing contacts, are you? That always makes it worse."

"No, no contacts. I'm OK," she managed.

"Do you want me to go splash him back?" Robin blushed as she thought how adorable it was that Scott was willing to defend her honor.

"No, but thank you for the offer," she smiled at him. "It's really sweet."

"I'm going to go jump in again," Scott decided. "See you ladies later." And he swam to the edge of the pool, pulling himself deftly out without the ladder.

Disappointed that he'd left, she turned to Hannah, who was grinning at her.

"What?" Robin asked her friend.

"Well, he certainly didn't come over here to talk to me!" Hannah squealed. "You go, girl!"

Soon Robin and Hannah were joined by another group of girls. Many of the boys were showing off on the diving boards, so the girls all laughed together and rated their skills. It was a while before Robin had the chance (and the courage) to talk to Scott again.

This time she was still in the shallow end, using an orca-shaped floatie to relax. Scott snuck up behind her and playfully grabbed the big whale floatie right out from under her. She squealed as she tried to get it back, but he held it just out of her arm's reach. He tossed it to one of his friends treading water nearby, and they played keep away from Robin as she tried to get it back. She hoped it wasn't too obvious that she always tried a little harder to get it back when Scott had it.

Finally, she pretended to give up and swim away. As soon as Scott was lulled into a false sense of security and looked away, she snuck back and grabbed the whale! Surprised, he grinned when he realized what she'd done and started to swim after her. He was clearly a better swimmer, but he allowed her to get a little head start. Another girl who was watching also desired some of Scott's attention, so she offered another floatie that she had, identical to the one Robin had just commandeered.

"I want the one she stole!" he exclaimed, and though he accepted the floatie, Scott continued to chase after Robin, who couldn't help but notice that the other girl looked crushed.

When Scott reached Robin, he wielded his orca like a sword and swung it at her orca. She parried, and they dueled for a few minutes, using their giant floaties as weapons. When they finally called a truce, they were both out of breath and laughing hard. They decided to each float using their own devices for a while and enjoyed some comfortable relaxation in silence.

All too soon, an announcement was made over the PA that it was time to head back to campus and for everyone to get out of the pool.

"Good night, Robin. See you later!" Scott said as he scrambled out of the pool and headed towards the men's room. Robin waited for him to disappear before using the ladder to climb out. She found Hannah and they headed into the locker room to shower off and change back into their street clothes.

Before they headed back to school, the buses stopped at a nearby Taco Bell. The principal passed out a few dollars of spending money to each student. Still basking in the excitement of the night, Robin didn't even mind standing in line for what seemed like forever for her treat. She felt a little bad for the store workers, whose eyes got big when they saw the buses and students pouring into their little fast food restaurant.

When she reached the cash register, she ordered her "regular" two bean burritos, minus the onions substitute tomatoes, because she knew that a teenage girl should never order onions. Having fresh breath was a priority when the possibility of running into that special someone existed!

It irked her a bit that Taco Bell charged extra for the tomatoes when she was just replacing the onions, but she paid her bill and grabbed several mild and green sauce packets and went to find her friends. She looked around for Scott and Richie, but they were nowhere to be seen.

As they pulled into campus, Hannah asked Robin, "Want to have a sleepover tonight in my room?"

"Of course!" Robin grinned, "I'll bring some sustenance."

After the bus parked and unloaded, the girls entered the dorm, bounding up the stairs each to their own rooms. Robin grabbed her pillow, blanket, and some snacks and headed to Hannah's room for some giggles and girl talk. After the RA checked them in, they talked late into the night about the evening they'd had, their hopes for the year, and, of course, their current crushes.

Robin couldn't stop talking about Scott, and Hannah had spent a lot of time at the pool talking to a junior boy named Derek. As they finally drifted off to sleep, Robin wondered if, perhaps, with the proper encouragement of Scott's attentions and a little luck, maybe she would not be "sweet sixteen and never been kissed" when her birthday rolled around next August.

CHAPTER 3
The Invitation

The next few days flew by for Robin. Though she was a good student, her sophomore classes were challenging and kept her busy. Being smart had never helped her make friends; in fact, in middle school it had seemed to do the opposite. During those years, she'd never had many close friends. In the small multi-grade classroom school, often the popular girls chose to pick on her, and the less popular girls didn't want to face being ostracized.

A particularly harsh realization of her social status came in fifth grade when one of the "popular" seventh-grade girls called her out-of-the-blue after school one day to chat. She'd said she needed to put Robin on speaker phone because she was multi-tasking and needed her hands free. Naively, Robin thought nothing of that; she had just been excited to be finally breaking into the "cool" crowd.

After several minutes of small talk, the older girl asked Robin who she liked. Robin hesitated for a moment but decided that this was her one chance at popularity, so she told her would-be friend who her current crush was. Immediately, she heard lots of giggling in the background. Apparently, there had been a secret audience to Robin's very private revelation. Crushed and discouraged, Robin quickly hung up the phone before she'd started to cry.

Fortunately, a new girl named Cora moved to the area the following year, and they developed a close friendship. Cora was at Sunnydale, too, and even though they were still friends, she had already become more popular than Robin, so the two girls didn't hang out as much anymore.

Even now, Robin felt like sometimes people befriended her only for homework help. She also knew they sometimes had the hope that she'd just let them copy her work. Even though she knew what they were after, she would never let someone just cheat off her work. This was most likely why she remained unpopular.

Scott never made her feel like a dork or used her for academic abilities, so she lived for the moments when she had time to talk to him. She was constantly reminded of a line from one of her favorite David Cook songs: "If you want to know the truth, you make or break my day." It was true. A kind word or two from Scott could turn even her bleakest day into a ray of sunshine.

On Monday, Robin was thrilled when she and Scott were assigned a joint project in Life Skills. That afternoon, they sat on a front campus bench "interviewing" students as they walked by about their opinion on whether or not the school should censor their email and other Internet activities like Facebook. Though every student agreed and did not think that they should be censored, Robin and Scott doubted that would help change any of the school's policies.

On Tuesday, they had to design geometric shapes in math class. Each student was encouraged to make a few unique shapes with white paper, then color and sign them. The collage would then be used for a bulletin board. Scott had forgotten his colored pencils at home. Robin was more than happy to share her crayons with him.

"Crayons?" Scott teased her with a twinkle in his eyes, "I love crayons! They make me feel like a kid again."

Robin blushed. She didn't admit that she still liked to use them in coloring books when she was feeling nostalgic. Her favorite memory from using crayons was using them to "write" on her family's old-fashioned wood stove in their living room. Watching the crayons melt into glorious bursts of color had been enthralling. Of course, she'd gotten in trouble, but it had been worth it.

She had been worried he'd be disappointed that she didn't have the more popular, "grown-up" (and more expensive) colored pencils. But as she watched him color with her supplies, she could tell he really didn't mind.

On Wednesday as the sophomores were transitioning between classes, Scott noticed the Koosh ball stored in her backpack's water bottle mesh pocket and grabbed it. Robin sometimes played with a colorful purple and green Koosh ball when she was journaling in English, or had free time to work on her homework in class. Lightly tossing or squeezing the colorful and soft toy helped her brainstorm. It was silly, she knew, but it worked. Her teachers had given her permission to use it, but they had warned her not to throw it to other students or to be distracting, or it would get taken away.

"Hey!" she protested.

"I haven't seen one of these in ages. And it's purple and green! Green is my favorite color," Scott informed her.

"You know, they were named because of the koosh sound they make when they hit the ground," she told him.

"I didn't know that."

"Give it back before I get into trouble," It was hard to be serious, but she thrust her hand out for him to return it before she got it taken away.

"I'll give it back," he said mischievously.

It was English, so they found their seats and pulled out their journals. The teacher had them free write for the first five minutes of every class. Most of the kids complained, but Robin loved to write and secretly looked forward to the daily assignment. All of a sudden her koosh ball landed on her journal. Startled and trying hard not to laugh, as it had indeed made a *koosh* sound, she looked up to see if the teacher had seen. Luckily, Ms. Cathey did not.

She looked over at Scott, who was grinning from ear to ear. When she was sure Ms. Cathey wasn't looking, she threw it back. And then a few minutes later, it landed back on her desk. Feeling very guilty but enjoying the attention, Robin continued to toss the koosh ball back and forth with Scott for the rest of the class period. Because Scott had played with it and since her favorite color was purple, the koosh ball was now extra special to Robin.

Even with all her flirtatious interactions with Scott, Robin was still unsure of what his feelings for her were. He hadn't asked her to hang out with him after class or for a weekend date, so maybe he just wanted to be friends. Weekend dates were the ultimate way to show off that you liked someone. If a boy asked a girl on one and she said yes, she was agreeing to sit with him at all the activities of the weekend: vespers, church, the Sabbath afternoon activity, and all meals!

Robin began to get her hopes up on Thursday night when Scott showed up halfway through evening Recreation. He and Richie didn't normally attend "Rec," but when he saw her, he sauntered over to say hello. The setting sun was bright, so she boldly asked if he'd block the sun for her. As he did, they talked about their classes and mutual friends for a few minutes.

"Did you ride with Richie?" Robin asked Scott. She knew he had because she'd watched them drive up, but she didn't want him to think she was stalking him.

"Yeah. He has a sweet ride," Scott said, referring to Richie's white Camaro parked nearby.

"It is a cool car," she agreed. "But why didn't he pick a brighter color? White is so hard to keep clean."

"Think about it. A white car for Richie *Snow*," Scott grinned.

Robin laughed. "I can't believe I hadn't made the connection! You're right. It is a perfect color for him."

Robin was letting her bangs grow out and had the long tendrils secured on each side of her head with a clip. Some of her hair was now getting in her eyes so she removed her clips to fix it. After she'd replaced one, Scott asked to see the second one and played with it between his thumb and one of his long fingers.

"This is pretty," he told her. Robin was very pleased he'd noticed. Each clip had a small flower with a green faux gem in the middle. She'd worn them because he'd told her his favorite color was green.

"Thanks," she smiled at him.

He continued to play with her hair clip as they sat together for a few minutes in companionable silence. Out of the blue, Scott asked her, "I think you're taller than me."

Surprised, it took a moment for her to answer. "I don't think I am. How tall are you?"

"Five eleven," he replied. "And you?"

"Probably five eight or nine."

"Good," he said. "I'm taller."

Robin blushed, and he changed the subject. *Does this mean he is interested in me, too?* She couldn't think of any other reason why he would care how tall she was. They watched the football intramural game for a few minutes, commenting on the good plays.

Even though it wasn't very girlie, Robin liked to play football and had spent many hours perfecting her catching skills with her dad. She could catch a "bullet," and her favorite pass was one where she had to jump a little and grab the ball with her hands stretched out over her head.

A few minutes before most students would be sent back to the dorms and the village students sent home, Scott mentioned that he was having a group over to his house on Saturday night to watch movies.

"That sounds like a lot of fun," Robin managed. *I hope that my response sounded natural.* She willed herself to calm down. *Please invite me*, she silently implored him.

He seemed to hesitate. "If you can get permission to get off campus, you should come."

Did he sound a little nervous as he said that? Robin wondered. *Or is it just wishful thinking?*

Aloud she said, "That sounds great! I'll talk to Becky tomorrow to see if I can go to her house after church on Sabbath!" Becky was a village sophomore who had been trying to get Robin to come to her house on a weekend.

The bell rang signaling the end of Rec, and they both stood up.

"See you tomorrow," Scott smiled at her and was gone.

Robin practically raced up the dorm steps, and as soon as she closed the door to her room, she grabbed her phone from her pocket and texted Becky. *Can I come to ur house Sat after church? Scott invited us to a party @ his house Sat nite!!*

It wasn't long before her phone pinged with Becky's response. *Just asked my parents. Sure! Eeek!*

The girls texted back and forth for a few more minutes and then Robin pulled out her geometry homework and tried to concentrate. It took her twice as long as normal to complete her assignment.

CHAPTER 4
The Milky Way

On Saturday morning, Robin awakened before her alarm. The plan was for her to go to church on campus with Becky and then afterward they would go to Becky's house to wait for Scott to call them. She spent extra time getting ready: picking out a dress (she borrowed one from Hannah), doing her hair (washed, dried, and pulled back with a cute clip), and putting on makeup (mascara, concealer, and lip gloss).

When she walked into the sanctuary, she spotted Becky and saw that she was saving her a seat. Disappointed that she didn't see Scott anywhere, she quickly sat down with her friend. It was a while into the service when Robin looked up to the balcony and spotted Scott with some other village students. Dorm students were not allowed to sit in the balcony until they were seniors. By default, this coveted privilege also extended to village students who were not under school rules at church even though the church building was technically on campus. There were also a few dorm kids who had signed out to local homes for the weekend.

Why is he sitting up there? Robin noticed several sophomore girls sitting near him including her longtime friend Cora, who had apparently signed out to Christina's house. *If he was interested in me, he could have sat down here.*

She tried to pay attention to the sermon, but she felt sick to her stomach. *But he did invite me to his house tonight,* she tried to remind herself.

After what seemed like an eternity, the congregation was standing for the closing hymn and the benediction. As the church emptied, Robin hung back with Becky's family, who were chatting with other church members. Robin couldn't hide her smile when she spotted Scott heading up the aisle towards them. She realized his mom had been sitting in the pew behind her. A cute little blonde girl jumped up and ran to his side.

"Hi, Robin!" Scott said and grinned down at the little girl next to him. "This is my niece, Susie. Say hi to Robin," he prompted her. She looked to be about four years old.

"Hi, Robin," the girl ducked her head behind Scott in shyness.

"Hello, Susie," Robin smiled encouragingly.

"Do you love your Uncle Scott?" her uncle asked her.

Susie grinned in response.

"I have two older sisters," Scott explained. "Susie is staying with us for a while." Robin had only known about Scott's older brother, a junior at Sunnydale. This was the first time she had heard about any other siblings.

Scott continued, "I just wanted to give you my cellphone number so that we can meet up this afternoon. A group of us are headed to Capen Park in Columbia to go rock climbing, but I'll text you and Becky when we get back so you can come over to my house. What is your number?"

As Robin rattled off her digits and he typed them in, she felt both a desire to get an invitation to go climbing and an intense relief that she hadn't been invited. She had never been rock climbing, but she knew from her family's trips to Colorado that she was completely and utterly terrified of heights. Whenever she reached the tree line, she became paralyzed with fear, unable to take one step higher up the trail. She was afraid she would roll off the mountain with nothing to grab hold of to slow her fall. Her mother had been forced to wait with her many times while her father and John summited whatever mountain peak they were climbing. Robin wasn't sure she could try climbing, even for Scott. But the invitation never came, so her internal conflict was for naught.

Her cellphone pinged signaling she had a new text. "Now you have my number," he said logically. "Well, I gotta go, but I'll let you know when I get back."

Scott took Susie's hand and led her back up the aisle and out of the sanctuary. Robin looked back at Becky, who signaled her that it was time to go. Becky's parents had been invited to Sabbath lunch at a senior girl's parents' house. After lunch, they entertained themselves looking at her old yearbooks and waiting for the text message. They also giggled as they looked at pictures taken on Becky's phone. After lunch the day before, while the girls had been hanging out on campus waiting for class, Becky started snapping shots. A few selfies had turned into an impromptu photo shoot of mostly Scott. Clearly embarrassed by the attention, he'd been a good sport about it for a few minutes before saying his cheeks were hurting from smiling. Even though Becky hadn't admitted it, Robin realized that she shared her crush with yet another girl.

It was late afternoon when Becky's parents declared it was time to head back to their house. And it was even later when Robin got the text from Scott, causing her to jump. Even though she told herself she clearly wasn't waiting for his text, her phone had remained in her hand or near her hand all afternoon.

We r back n town, the text read. *Should I pick u girls up n an hour?* Even though Scott didn't have his license yet, he did have his permit and only lived a mile from Becky, so it was probably OK that he came and picked them up, Robin reasoned.

She was ready to go that minute, but she texted him back that an hour was fine and that they would see him soon. The girls could hardly contain their excitement as the minute hand of the clock slowly moved around. It was nearly sunset when the girls spotted an old pickup headed down the driveway to Becky's house.

Even though Robin knew her permission slip was to be off campus with Becky's family, she was willing to take a risk, and they ran out the door to meet him. Robin reached the passenger door of the truck first, and she climbed onto the bench seat with a little smugness realizing that she'd have to sit close to Scott for all three of them to fit. Becky looked disappointed but smiled anyway.

When they arrived at the house, Scott insisted on giving Robin and Becky a quick tour and introduced them to his mom. Then the three of them headed up to the loft where the movie would be. Scott's phone rang and Robin could tell that someone asked him about getting the movie.

"Richie's outside, and we have to run to Redbox and pick a movie. I'll be back soon," he said, apologetically. Soon Robin and Becky found themselves alone with Scott's cat and Susie, who had found her way upstairs.

At least I like kids and cats, Robin mused. Susie didn't waste any time. She told Robin about her cat, her stuffed animals, and her favorite color. Soon Susie was called downstairs for bedtime, and Robin realized how much she had enjoyed the time with the small, and now considerably less shy, child.

Other people started arriving and by the time Scott was back with a few movies, there were ten people in the loft: five guys and five girls. Richie was there as well as Scott's brother, Paul. There were two other guys: a village junior named Aaron and a dorm sophomore named Jack. Cora was there with Christina, and Christina's older sister, Angie. Robin got a sinking feeling as she connected the dots. It looked like Cora had eyes only for Jack, but why were Christina and Angie there? *Scott sat with Christina at church, and she's here now*, she tried to shake off the feeling that it was more than a coincidence. It was clear that the rest of the group had all been at Capen Park climbing all afternoon, and again Robin felt an internal conflict between her fear of heights and her desire to spend more time with Scott and Richie.

Everyone settled down to watch the movie and eat popcorn. Robin wasn't next to Scott; she was seated between Becky and Paul. But thankfully, Christina wasn't next to Scott either. She was next to Aaron and Cora. The boys had picked a new comedy, and there were several parts that made Robin laugh so hard she started crying. Another part had some innuendo that embarrassed her, and she could feel her face getting hot.

Richie looked over at her and grinned. "Don't watch the movie. Watch the girls! Red Robin, mmm," he teased her.

At some point someone started passing around a two-liter bottle of frozen Mountain Dew. Even though Robin didn't really like drinking after other people, or drinking soda for that matter, especially something caffeinated like Mountain Dew, she didn't want to be rude. So she grabbed the bottle after Scott and took a few obligatory sips. She was surprised at how good it tasted.

After the movie ended, Robin glanced at her watch and saw that it was a few minutes after eleven. If she didn't leave soon, she'd be late for her midnight curfew. The other dorm students weren't expected back, but she had only signed out for the day. Awkwardly, she mentioned to Scott that she and Becky needed to get back to Becky's house. Then someone in her family could take them back to the dorm.

"No problem. I can take you and Becky back to her house,"he said and turned to the others. "Go ahead and start the next movie. I'll be back soon."

Becky was going to stay with another girl in the dorm, so she had brought a small backpack with her. The three of them grabbed their stuff and headed back outside to the truck. Robin felt a tiny bit guilty as she edged Becky out for the middle seat again. On the way to his house, Scott had turned the music up. This time, he turned it low so they could talk.

"If the truck's roof wasn't there, you could see the Milky Way," Scott told the girls. "It's showing up really good this week. There are so many stars that they just look like a milky band," he explained.

With admiration at his astronomical knowledge, both Robin and Becky assured him they would look when they got out. When they reached Becky's house, all the lights in the house were out.

"Can you take us back to the dorm?" Becky asked.

"As long as you don't tell anyone I drove that far without my license," Scott said. "I'm not supposed to be on the highway without an adult." Robin and Becky nodded their consents.

Robin couldn't be sure, but it seemed like Scott was sitting a little closer to her this time. And he certainly didn't have to bump her knee each time he shifted gears in the manual transmission, but she didn't mind one bit. All too soon the ride ended. Robin and Becky waved goodbye to Scott as they headed into the dorm.

CHAPTER 5
Monday Memories

Normally Sundays were fun for Robin, but this time, the day dragged on and on. She couldn't wait to go to class and see Scott again. On Monday morning Robin woke up with a smile on her face. She didn't need to hit snooze, and she hummed softly to herself as she showered and dressed for class.

Life Skills would be in the cafeteria today. They were going to learn how to make gluten. The class had been divided into two groups, and she would go today and have a free period tomorrow. Fortunately, Scott was signed up for Monday, too.

When she arrived to class, she looked around for Scott but didn't see him. When he arrived a few minutes late, he smiled at her, and her face lit up. It was hard to concentrate on dipping the gluten in the milk and bread when all she could think of was Scott.

After class as they were walking to the Ad building to head to chapel, Scott playfully pushed her off the sidewalk. "I just can't seem to stay on the sidewalk," he grinned.

Robin laughed, "Try harder!" And she pushed him off the other side.

After chapel, Robin went to work in the office. When she updated the daily lunch menu, it took her twice as long as normal. She had to concentrate extra carefully every time she answered the phone. "Sunnydale Academy, this is Robin. How may I help you?" It was just so hard not to think about Scott!

During work, she ran an errand to the library and was pleased to run into Richie. They chatted a few minutes about the fun they'd had on Saturday night. He teased her again about blushing, and they laughed when the librarian had to "shush" them. Grinning at him, she waved and headed back to the office.

She had a free period right before lunch and went outside to study for her Biology test on Wednesday. She sat on the bench nearest the cafeteria and was rewarded when Scott came over to sit next to her after he got off work. He asked to look at her notes, and they pretended to study. He was sitting cross-legged on the bench, and his knee was touching her leg. Robin blushed as she thought it might be more appropriate if they were studying chemistry.

"Hey Scott!" a freshman girl called from across campus, "I need to talk to you."

Scott looked confused but got up and walked over to Cindy. He and Cindy talked for a few minutes and then he came back to the bench laughing and sat back down next to Robin. Though she was dying to know what they had talked about, she didn't ask. When it was time to eat lunch, she and Scott walked to the cafeteria together.

The line was long, and when they reached the cashier, Scott realized he had forgotten his lunch money. He flashed Samantha, another sophomore, his million-dollar grin. "Can I pay you tomorrow?"

"Well… I'm not really supposed to," she hesitated, "but… OK." How could anyone resist his charms?

Robin and Scott got their food and found a table near a window. Robin was taking a seat across from him when Scott noticed Robin's water.

"You have to try my grape soda!" he urged.

She started to protest that she didn't normally drink soda, but that hadn't stopped her on Saturday night. She took a sip. "That's pretty good," she conceded.

"See, you should trust me more often!"

Scott looked like he might say more, but Becky joined them. She took a seat across from Robin. Scott asked Becky how the rest of her weekend had been.

"Not very good," Becky admitted. "We found out yesterday that my cousin died on Saturday afternoon in a motorcycle accident."

"Oh, I am so sorry to hear that," Robin said. She felt sad for her friend.

"If he loved riding his bike, the important thing is that he died having fun," Scott decided.

"When is the funeral?" Robin asked.

"It's Thursday," Becky said. "He lived two hours away, but since it is home leave later this week, I won't have to miss class that day."

"Were you close?" Robin asked.

"He was a lot older than I am, so we weren't super close, but I just saw him at the family reunion this summer. It's so weird to think that he's gone."

"If I died, I wouldn't want my friends to come to my funeral," Scott said, surprising them with his comment.

"But going to a funeral gives people closure," Robin reasoned.

"I would want people to remember me the way I was when I was alive," Scott insisted.

"That makes sense too, but I think it's up to the individual. Becky, do what you need to do for your cousin," Robin encouraged.

Soon others joined them, and the topic changed. They ate the rest of their lunch and headed to the Ad building for class. During Bible, the teacher let everyone work on their homework outside. It was a really nice day, so it was hard to focus on the homework. Robin wanted to listen to the birds singing… and talk to Scott, of course.

At one point Scott stood up. "Girls, gather round!"

Most of the sophomore girls gathered around to hear his important announcement. When he had their undivided attention, Scott announced, "Look, I'm popular with the girls!"

Laughing, everyone returned to their Bible assignment.

During Biology, Scott nudged her with his knee. "How'd you like Saturday night?"

"It was fun!" Robin replied.

"And how did you like the ride back?" Scott winked at her.

Robin thought of how close they had been on the bench seat in his truck and blushed. "You are a good driver. And I liked your truck."

With great discipline, she turned back to listen to their teacher, Mr. Jones, as he lectured about mitosis. *PMAT*, she told herself, *Prophase, Metaphase, Anaphase, and Telophase, I need to focus for the test on Wednesday!*

They had to take a test in English, so she couldn't talk to Scott, and she didn't sit next to him in Geometry or History, so it was a relief when the last bell rang and the class emptied out into the hall and onto front campus. She spotted him outside talking to Christina, and her jealousy instantly flared. She decided to head into the dorm to drop her backpack off in her room. In the hallway, she ran into Hannah.

"Did you hear?" Hannah wasted no time before questioning Robin.

"Hear what?" Robin asked.

"Cindy Richardson asked Scott who he liked today!"

"So that's what she asked him. Scott and I were studying Biology, and Cindy told him she had to talk to him. What did he say?"

"He said he liked a sophomore!" Hannah squealed.

"Well, that doesn't mean me…" Robin tried to stay rational.

At that moment, another girl came down the hall. Hannah and Robin stopped talking because it was no secret that Stephanie liked Scott, too. Robin had suspected that Stephanie liked Scott when she had offered him the whale floatie at the pool and pouted when he didn't give her his undivided attention or any attention at all, really. However, in the last few days the rumor mill had confirmed that Stephanie and Robin did indeed share a mutual love interest. But Stephanie did not pass Robin and Hannah by as expected. Instead, she stopped and said to Robin, "You make me sick!"

"What?" Robin was taken aback.

"Scott is looking for you," Stephanie said angrily before walking past them and slamming her door.

Hannah and Robin looked at each other and grinned. "You'd better go talk to him!" Hannah urged.

"See you later!" Robin called as she practically skipped down the hall.

Outside, it took Robin a few minutes to spot Scott. He was playing hacky sack with Richie and a few other guys. When Richie and Scott saw her, they both waved. She stood watching nearby but didn't try and join in. Her skills hadn't improved much since the last time they had played, and she was sure their companions would not have as much patience. After a few more minutes, Richie pulled his phone out of his pocket and checked the time.

Turning to Scott, he said, "If you still want a ride home, we need to leave now."

"See you in the morning, Robin!" Scott grinned at her as the two of them walked away. She was disappointed at the missed opportunity to talk to both of them but told herself she'd get a chance tomorrow. She watched Richie's Camaro drive past front campus.

He sure does like to drive fast, she noted.

Since Richie and Scott were gone, Robin headed back to the dorm to study for her Biology test. During "Relaxed Study Hall," Robin hung out with Hannah. Hannah was quick to inform her that she'd heard more gossip that people thought it was either Robin or Christina that Scott liked.

"Christina did go to his house on Saturday night, and he was talking to her after class. *But* he signed up for the gluten and bread days in Life Skills right after me. He could have chosen the days with Christina, but he chose to spend them with me," Robin rationalized.

"And he was looking for you this afternoon…" Hannah added.

"I guess time will tell. I hope it's me!" Robin crossed her fingers.

Back in her room for "Strict Study Hall," Robin finished her homework early that night. She resisted the urge to text Scott to see what he was doing, but she did check his Facebook page to see if he'd posted any updates. When she saw that there was nothing

A few minutes after 9 p.m., the power suddenly went out. new, she decided to write in her journal, and of course, her writing was mostly about Scott. She wondered what he was doing, and if he was thinking about her, too. A few minutes after 9 p.m., the power suddenly went out.

That's odd, Robin thought. *I wonder what happened.* It wasn't too long before the power came back on, so she dismissed the question and went back to thinking about Scott. She drifted off to sleep that night still wondering if he was thinking about her.

PART TWO

A Time for Tears

"Rejoice with those who rejoice,
and weep with those who weep"
(Rom. 12:15).

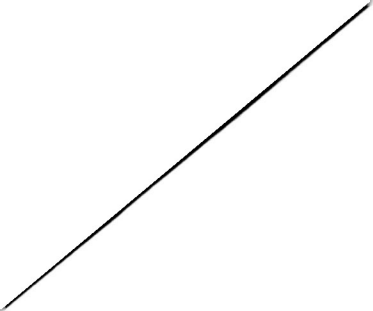

CHAPTER 6
The Nightmare Begins

Robin got up early Tuesday morning to type a paper. She tended to procrastinate, and it was due that day, so she turned her phone on silent and determined not to check her Facebook account or her email until she was done. Since she had attended the kitchen class yesterday, she did not have class this morning. She planned to use the extra hour to finish her paper. At least Scott wouldn't be there, so she wasn't missing any time with him.

Concentrating deeply on her assignment, Robin didn't hear the first knock on the door. The second knock was much louder, so Robin quickly headed to the door. She was surprised to see Hannah standing on the other side because she was supposed to be in class herself.

"Why haven't you answered any of my texts?" Hannah demanded. But she didn't look angry, only sorrowful. Robin could tell by her red eyes that she had been crying.

"I turned my phone on silent so that I wouldn't be distracted. What's wrong?"

"I don't know how to tell you this," Hannah's eyes filled with tears. "But Scott and Richie were in a car accident last night. We found out at breakfast."

Robin felt like she had been punched in the stomach with an iron fist.

"Are they OK?" It was hard to force the words out.

Hannah shook her head, and the tears flowed harder.

"No," she choked. She took a deep breath. "Scott didn't make it," she swallowed hard and took another deep breath, "and Richie might not either."

Robin couldn't breathe. Her body felt numb, and she barely noticed that she and Hannah had been joined by the assistant girls' dean, Miss Tanner. *This cannot be real*, she told herself.

"Robin, Dr. Cunningham is in the lobby," Miss Tanner said, gently. "He'd like to speak with you."

"OK." Her voice was barely above a whisper. *Why does the principal want to talk to me?*

As she followed the assistant dean down the hall, Miss Tanner asked her if she'd heard about the accident. Robin nodded. It felt like someone else was walking down the hall, someone else hearing about the accident.

It has to be a nightmare, she wanted to scream. *But if it was, why does it feel so real? Why am I not waking up?*

> *It has to be a nightmare, she wanted to scream. But if it was, why does it feel so real? Why am I not waking up?*

As she entered the dorm lobby, she saw Dr. Cunningham stand up to greet her.

"I am so sorry to tell you, but Richie Snow and Scott Hayes were in an automobile accident. Last night around 9 p.m. Richie's car veered off the road and hit a telephone pole."

So that's why the power went out, Robin realized.

He hesitated and continued, "Scott was killed instantly, and Richie is at the hospital in critical condition. I understand you were dating Scott?"

"No," Robin whispered, her voice barely audible. "But I wanted to..."

"I am very sorry for your loss. We will have grief counselors available today if you want to talk to someone." Dr. Cunningham patted her shoulder and headed out of the dorm.

Robin felt her legs go weak, but she suddenly found herself surrounded by Hannah and some of her other friends. They took her hands and together they went outside to the flagpole where a group had gathered to pray for Richie's and Scott's families. Even though the mid-September day was uncharacteristically warm, Robin felt cold, like she was swimming in icy water. She hadn't felt this cold since she'd done the ALS ice bucket challenge last summer. She asked Hannah to get her a jacket, but another friend quickly offered her an oversized sweatshirt. Robin put it on, but even with its added warmth, she felt no better and could not stop shaking.

Home leave had been scheduled to start Wednesday after classes, but an emergency early start was called, and classes were canceled for the rest of the week. Several teachers told Robin and her friends that grief counselors were available to anyone who wanted to talk.

A bus took students to the hospital to pray for Richie. Since they had been told that Richie was in a coma, Robin couldn't bear to face the possibility that he would probably die as well, so she stayed on campus. Besides, Robin didn't know what to pray. She had attended Christian schools her whole life, and while she had memorized many Bible texts in Sabbath School and Pathfinders, she realized now that she didn't really have a deep personal relationship with God. But now, oh how she wished she did!

She and Hannah walked around the Square, the nickname of the path around the perimeter of campus. They didn't speak, but they took comfort in each other's presence.

That afternoon Robin's mom came and picked her up. She gave her a big hug. "I am so, so sorry," she said.

Robin nodded, but she knew her mom could not really understand the intensity of her pain. "Thanks for coming to get me so quickly," Robin said, quietly. "I just want to go home."

During the forty-five minute drive back to their house, Robin received the dreaded text from Hannah. Richie was gone, too. Robin covered her face with her hands and cried. Her mom didn't say anything, and when Robin finally looked up, she could tell she had also been crying.

At home, Robin lay down on her bed and just stared at the ceiling for hours. She pinched herself. It hurt. She wasn't dreaming. She wasn't going to wake up. After a while she decided to try and write in her journal. Maybe it would help to write down what she was feeling.

Staring at the blank page, Robin thought about death. Even at fifteen, Robin was no stranger to loss. She had been close to her paternal great-grandmother when she had died of a heart attack and at eight years old Robin had been devastated to learn that she would no longer be able to play with her friend. And even though she hadn't really understood why, she had been shocked to learn that her great-grandma was cold when she went to touch her in the casket.

After that, it had been years before death struck close to Robin's heart again. But just that spring, her friend Timothy had lost his little sister and mother in just a little over a week. Tim's mom had been sick with cancer for a while and had been away for treatments. On the day his mom arrived home, friends of the family dropped Tim's seven-year-old sister off at home after school. In her excitement to see her mother, Libby hadn't looked both ways before crossing the street and had been struck by an oncoming car. She had died on the way to the hospital.

At Libby's funeral visitation, Robin and her mother had found themselves in line with the couple who had driven the car that had hit her. It had all been a crazy misfortune of being at the wrong place at the wrong time. They only drove that particular road once or twice a year. They hadn't been speeding, but she had just jumped out in front of them, and they'd had no time to react. The man had swerved, almost missing her but striking her with the front right side of the car. They were so sorry. Robin and her mom had tried their best to reassure the nice couple that it hadn't been their fault.

Libby's mom had been devastated at the loss and took an immediate turn for the worse. Eight days after Libby's funeral, Robin had found herself at the funeral for Tim's mom. Such a profound loss for a family of six now reduced to a family of four. And now less than six months later, here she was staring another tragedy in the face.

Life, she finally wrote, *is so unfair. Why did little Libby die when she was so young and full of life? Why did her mother have to suffer so? And why God, have you allowed Richie and Scott to die now? They were the only guys that were nice to me. I need,* she paused, crossed the word out and wrote, *needed them. If only one of them had died, I would have the other to comfort me. But they are both gone. What am I supposed to do? How will I ever get over this?*

Robin thought about the last conversations she'd had with Richie and Scott. She'd been lucky to see Richie at the library yesterday, and they'd had a good time, as usual, talking and laughing together. Then she thought about Scott. *The last time I talked to him was after drama yesterday,* she wrote. *He was wearing an orange U-Haul hat, his green cargo pants, and his green Boone County Fire Department polo. All green, his favorite. He'll never smile at me again, that genuine smile that lit up his whole face. And his eyes, so green with such a depth that I'll never get to understand.*

Robin wondered how the accident had happened. Though he had been notorious for driving fast, Richie had been a good driver. Had there been something in the road making Richie swerve and causing the car to hit the telephone pole? Had they been wearing their seatbelts or had they been ejected from the car? Had it been like the song by Pearl Jam she'd heard a few times on the radio where the crash came with "screamin' tires and bustin' glass"? She hoped that it all had been quick and that they had not been scared.

Looking back at her entry from the night before, her eyes fell on the last line: *I wonder if Scott's thinking about me, too.*

He hadn't been thinking about her. He'd already been dead. As she looked over her other journal entries since school began, nearly every page made some kind of mention of or reference to Scott.

"Oh, Scott, were you having fun?" she cried.

Tears blurred her vision, and she couldn't write anymore. As she lay on her bed and sobbed, her heart felt like it would break. Soon a warm body pressed up

> Tears blurred her vision, and she couldn't write anymore. As she lay on her bed and sobbed, her heart felt like it would break.

next to her. It began to purr.

She snuggled Smokey, her big gray cat, close to her and said to him, "You seem to understand, buddy. You know I'm sad, and you just want to help. But there's nothing anyone can do."

CHAPTER 7
An Emotional Deluge

On Wednesday morning Robin awoke and for a second felt panicked about her Biology test. Then she remembered the test was postponed until next week. And then she remembered why. She started shaking uncontrollably again. She stumbled through the morning and numbly accepted an invitation to go hang out with Cora and a few friends at the Columbia Mall. Maybe once she got there, she'd realize it was all some big mistake and that Scott and Richie weren't really gone after all.

When she arrived at the mall, it was obvious Cora and Jack had started dating Saturday night. They greeted her happily with hands intertwined. And Sandy was there! Sandy was Scott's ex-girlfriend and apparently had gone home with Cora so that she could attend the funerals on Friday. Robin felt sick to her stomach and regretted her decision to venture out.

It's not like I could really pretend it hadn't happened, she reminded herself. *But oh, how I wish I could wake up from this nightmare that is now my life!*

Since it was lunchtime, the four friends headed to the Food Court to get some food. Using some of her hard-earned babysitting money,

Robin ordered two regular bean burritos from Taco Bell. No need to forgo onions this time. She wouldn't be kissing anyone anytime soon.

As they ate, Jack tried to cheer her up. "It should ruin your day but not your week!"

She knew he didn't mean it the way it sounded, but his words seemed cold and callous.

What does he care? His words caused anger to stir up within Robin. *He and Cora are alive and able to spend time together. He just doesn't understand. Maybe he can pretend it didn't happen, but I can't!*

Later Cora and Jack disappeared, and Robin found herself walking around with Sandy. It wasn't so bad until they ran into Mrs. Hayes and a few other ladies coming out one of the major department stores. Mrs. Hayes looked like a zombie, but she acknowledged both girls by name. Sandy informed Scott's mother how much she missed her son. Robin tried to say something sympathetic, but her mouth felt like cotton, and she couldn't say anything. One of the ladies, a teacher from the school, pulled Robin aside and explained they were shopping for Scott's last clothes.

"Oh," Robin's voice sounded hollow. "I'm so sorry."

Mrs. Hayes and the ladies wandered off. Sandy pointed to a boutique she wanted to go in, seemingly unfazed by the conversation. Robin pointed to a chair in the corridor and sat down to wait for her. She couldn't help breaking down and sobbing right there in the middle of the mall.

When Sandy returned, she informed Robin that the store clerk had asked if she was OK.

"I think I'm a little better now. It was just so hard running into Mrs. Hayes."

"Well, it shouldn't have been that hard for you," Sandy said, annoyed. "I'm the one that dated Scott. You liked him, but I loved him."

Sandy's words stung. *But you didn't talk to him at all this year. My life is the one that has changed.* Robin's heart ached, but she said nothing.

Robin had one shopping goal for the day. She wanted to buy gel pens to write letters to put in Scott's and Richie's caskets. She directed Sandy to a shop that sold writing supplies and carefully selected two pretty pens: one purple and one green. Green for Scott's favorite color, and she'd learned yesterday that purple had been Richie's favorite color. *Just like me,* she thought.

The two girls continued wandering around the mall and finally met up with Jack and Cora. Jack and Cora looked flushed and happy. It made Robin sick to her stomach. After more awkward conversation, Robin got a text message. She looked at her phone and had never been so glad to read the text that her mom was outside waiting to pick her up. She pasted a smile on her face and waved goodbye to the three and walked out to meet her mom in the parking lot.

"Hey Pumpkin Eater, did you have a good time?" Robin's mom asked as she climbed into the front passenger seat.

Even though she was fifteen, most of the time the nickname was endearing. Today it annoyed her, so she snapped, "I'm not a baby. Don't call me that! I don't want to talk about it."

Robin's mom looked unsure, but she remained silent for the rest of the ride home. When they got home, Robin slammed the door as she got out of the car and headed into the house.

Surely this isn't my life, she told herself. But as she walked past her dad who was watching the local edition of Fox News, she was reminded again that it was.

"A second Boone County teenager died yesterday from injuries sustained in a car accident on Monday night on Route V near Hallsville." Robin's eyes were now glued to the screen.

The reporter continued, "Seventeen-year-old Richard Snow was pronounced dead at 1:15 p.m. on Tuesday at Boone Hospital here in Columbia." A picture of Richie's smiling face from last year's school portrait flashed on the screen.

"Although firefighters responded to the one-car accident within minutes, fifteen-year-old Scott Hayes was pronounced dead at the scene." Now a picture of Scott, one that Robin hadn't seen before, was being shown.

"Speed was determined to be the major factor in the accident. Richard was from Clark and Scott was from Sturgeon. Visitation will be tomorrow night from 5-8 p.m. at the Fenton Funeral

Chapel in Centralia, and the funeral is on Friday at 11 a.m. at the Sunnydale Adventist Academy Church. It's time to take a break, but when we return…. "

Robin couldn't breathe. She forced herself to walk calmly to her room where she locked the door behind her. Once again she threw herself onto her bed and sobbed as if her heart was breaking.

An hour later her mom knocked on the door to tell her dinner was ready.

"I'm not hungry," Robin called through the door, even though she could smell the food and knew her mom had prepared one of her favorite meals.

"We will save you some if you change your mind," her mom said. She sounded sad but didn't press the issue like she normally would have.

A thought kept nagging Robin. On the very day he had died, Scott had told Robin and Becky that if he died, he would want his friends to remember him the way he was and not to go to his funeral. So should she go? Or should she not go? He hadn't known he had hours left on the earth when he had said that, but should she honor his wishes?

Robin realized that she needed advice. And she knew the best person she could ask was someone who had recently experienced loss himself. She and Tim had grown close over the summer months. After his sister and mother had died, Robin had tried to be there for him, never asking about his loss but just listening whenever he needed to talk. He had a crush on Cora, so that was always a safe topic. And even though she hadn't talked to him since she had been back in school, she knew he wouldn't mind a call. So she dialed his number and waited for him to answer. Because she didn't want to cause Tim any pain, she was nervous to bring up the topic, and it seemed her heartbeat was almost as loud as the telephone's rings.

"How's my girl?" Having looked at his caller-ID, Tim answered cheerfully. Robin blushed even though she knew he didn't mean it *that* way. At one point she had entertained those thoughts towards him, but he had always been more than clear that he liked Cora.

So now he was just a really nice and safe, guy friend.

"Not too good," she admitted, and the story spilled out. Tim listened carefully as she explained her inner conflict between the lunch conversation and her desire to attend the funeral for some closure.

"I think you should go," he finally answered. "Scott wouldn't have wanted people to miss his funeral if it was important to them. And from what you have just told me, I think you will regret not going. Besides, he hadn't known he was going to die. We all say things sometimes that we wouldn't mean if we knew it meant hurting someone's feelings to do it."

"Thank you, Tim," Robin said. She felt a surge of relief. "You have been so good to me," she continued. "I want you to know your friendship means a lot."

"Back at you, Robin!" Sensing the need for a mood change in their conversation, Tim continued, "So what's Cora up to these days?"

They continued their conversation for another ten minutes or so. Tim was disappointed to hear that Cora seemed to be interested in Jack, but he remained optimistic about their potential future someday. He even made Robin laugh a few times. By the time she hit the "end call" button, she had almost forgotten what had happened. Almost.

She contemplated going out to spend time with her family, but she knew she had behaved badly and just couldn't face them. She sat on her bed and stared at the wall. After a while she heard another soft knock on her door.

"It's John," her brother's muffled voice came through the still locked door. "I was just wondering if you might want Smokey again tonight."

Her brother was never one to share the cat, so the gesture touched Robin's heart. She wiped her eyes and crossed the room to unlock the door.

"Thanks," she said as John awkwardly passed her the large, fluffy, purring cat. She left the door slightly ajar so Smokey could leave if he

Her brother was never one to share the cat, so the gesture touched Robin's heart.

needed to use the litter box and snuggled him close as she sobbed herself into another fitful sleep.

CHAPTER 8
Reminiscing

Robin slept in as long as she could on Thursday. In her dreams, Scott and Richie were still alive, and the world was right again. It was reality that had become the nightmare. When she finally dragged herself out of bed, she decided to log into Facebook and spent an hour reading the memories that others had posted on Scott's and Richie's pages and added some of her own.

Through her tears, she wrote about how Richie had blamed her for all the rides shutting down when they had both gone with a group to Six Flags last year. She laughed in spite of herself as she remembered how Richie had entertained their small crowd with his antics when they had suddenly found themselves stuck on a ride. The ride had failed to return to the exit platform, and even though they were only a foot off the ground, they had been instructed to remain on the ride until the problem was fixed. The park staff did not want to risk the liability of anyone twisting an ankle. Later, when another ride shut down right before it was their turn to ride, Richie had teased her that she was bad luck. He couldn't keep a straight face even as he said it, so she had known it was all in good fun.

She described how Richie had liked to scare her and others by hiding his pet hedgehog in an anatomy skull and having it pop out and how he was always such a good sport in games. She remembered how during last year's track and field, he'd been winning one of the races when a fellow runner fell. He had stopped and helped his competitor up before continuing the race. He'd placed third, but everyone knew he deserved the first place spot.

She also remembered times he'd tickled her when she didn't want to tell him something or she had candy he wanted. And their snowball fights and stare downs. His bright blue eyes had been so alluring; she'd always look away first because she was afraid he could read her thoughts. She'd had a big crush on him last year, even after he'd started dating a junior girl, but she transitioned into considering him one of her best friends. Those private memories she kept to herself.

On Scott's page she wrote about how he had told her and Becky about the Milky Way on Saturday night. They had all been blissfully unaware and carefree as they watched the movies, laughing together as they drank the no longer fizzy soda. They certainly wouldn't have been so nonchalant had they known that in two days Scott and Richie would be gone forever. But they hadn't known, so they'd been able to have their unadulterated fun. She would always treasure that special time with her friends. Would her soul ever be able to feel pure joy like that again?

She continued writing on Scott's Facebook page and explained that he often had chosen to drink grape soda at lunch because it reminded him of children's medicine and how he and Richie had tried valiantly to teach her to play hacky sack. She told of how she'd seen Scott leave his group of friends to sit with a girl who was sitting by herself at vespers and how he had been so good with Susie and how she had adored him. It was obvious from the Facebook messages that everyone had adored him, just like everyone had adored Richie.

She spent the rest of the morning working on her letters. She wrote draft after draft, agonizing over her final messages to her friends. She told them how much they had meant to her and how much she'd miss them. She wrote about some of her favorite memories with them, some of the ones she'd included on Facebook, but most of the memories in her letters were private. She also thanked them for being so nice to her. Finally, she was satisfied with her work, so she carefully copied both letters onto nice stationery using the gel pens.

She decided to give Scott the green flower from her hair clip. He had asked to keep it after he had played with it that day at Rec, a day which now seemed long ago. But she hadn't given it to him. It had become a treasured reminder of their interaction, and she had played with it so much afterward that the flower had fallen off the clip. Her letter to Scott closed with the line: *I'm sorry I wouldn't let you have the clip when you asked, but I'm giving the flower to you now. Since I'll have the other one, I'll always feel close to you when I look at it.*

She folded each letter into thirds and placed them into envelopes. After sealing them, she wrote each boy's name on the front and put them into her purse, so she wouldn't forget them when they left for the visitation that night.

During lunch, Robin's mom asked her if she wanted to leave for the visitation a little early so they could visit the accident site. Robin threw her arms around her mom's neck in response. "I'd like that," she said.

Later that afternoon, Robin and her mother left for Centralia with plenty of time to stop at the accident site on the way. As they were driving down the road the accident had occurred on, Robin wondered aloud if they would be able to find the right spot. She need not have worried; it was soon clear exactly where her friends had spent their last lucid moments.

As they rounded a corner, they could see debris all along the side of the road. The totaled car had been removed, but there were still bits of broken glass from the windows and some fiberglass from the car's body, and miscellaneous wires were strewn about everywhere. The telephone pole that was hit had been replaced, but the broken one still lay beside the road waiting for pickup.

Her mom parked their car in a safe spot, and she and Robin walked around the accident site in silent reverence. Robin examined the curve in the road. It didn't look that bad, but she'd heard that they had been driving around 105 miles per hour. At that speed, everything is a lot more difficult to navigate. And if something had run onto the road....

What really happened that night? Robin asked herself. But she knew that with both witnesses to the accident gone, she would never get to find out.

When her mom finally said they needed to go, she suggested Robin take some pieces of the wreckage for keepsakes. So Robin lingered over her selection and finally chose a piece of white fiberglass, a plastic piece from what she assumed had been the bumper, and some wire fragments. They again drove in silence into town.

Even though they had arrived a little early, the visitation line at the funeral was already quite long. Robin noticed a wide diversity in the people standing in line waiting to pay their final respects to Scott and Richie: teenagers like her, adults who had obviously come straight from work, people dressed all in black who must be family members, and even some Amish families.

Scott did live out by some of their farms, Robin remembered.

Normally Robin loved how Amish people made her think of the olden days. Their transportation, their "plain" attire, and their self-sufficient way of living had declared that modern life didn't need to be as fast paced as it was. Today their presence was just another reminder of why today wasn't normal. *Were they coming to support the hurting mothers in their community or had they interacted with Scott and been given a glimpse of how special he was? Just how many lives did he and Richie touch?*

As Robin and her mother entered the building, Becky flung herself into Robin's arms. She had mascara running down her cheeks, and her eyes were bloodshot and swollen. *She's been faring about as well as me,* Robin noticed. *I made a good choice not to wear any makeup.*

"Have you seen them?" Robin asked Becky.

"Yes. They look horrible!" Becky's eyes watered again, and she thrust an envelope into Robin's hands. "Here, these are for you. I made triples." Robin realized that Becky had printed the pictures they had taken together just the week before.

"Thank you!" Robin said as her own eyes filled with tears. Robin's gratitude was overwhelming at the thoughtfulness of her friend. She flipped through the pictures stopping at one where Scott was not looking at the camera.

He was looking at me, she realized. She knew this particular picture would forever be her favorite one of him.

As they waited in line, Robin could see the caskets and sometimes she could see the two heads peeking out. She could tell Richie wore a baseball hat but other than that she couldn't really see them. She was thankful for that because, as it was, it was hard for her not to run screaming from the room.

As they greeted the families, Robin's mother asked permission for Robin to put her letters in the caskets and both sets gave their consent. Robin had begged her mom to do that since she knew it would be too hard to ask for herself.

Richie's brother told Robin that Richie had considered her a really close friend. She was touched, but the knowledge, precious as it was, seemed to make her feel even worse. Had she been a good friend to him? She hoped so. She told his brother that she had considered him a really close friend, too.

Mrs. Hayes hugged Robin and Becky. She told them she still wanted them to visit even though Scott was gone. Both girls nodded their agreement.

"Everyone loved Scott," Robin told Mrs. Hayes.

"What was not to love?" Mrs. Hayes replied.

"Mrs. Hayes, Robin and I took these pictures last week. We would like you to have these copies," Becky said, passing an envelope to Scott's mother.

Mrs. Hayes hugged the envelope to her chest and thanked the girls for their kindness.

Then the line moved Robin away from the families and to the boys themselves. As she peered into each casket, she was shocked. They did not look real! Richie's face was puffy, and it looked like his lips had been cut. Robin knew the puffiness was probably because Richie's parents had chosen to donate his organs. Robin saw numerous bruises on Scott's arms and neck despite the mortician's best efforts to conceal them with makeup. It was so painful looking at the waxen-like shells of her friends—Robin's knees went wobbly.

Being careful not to bump either one, Robin managed to place her letters into each young man's coffin before racing out of the room to compose herself. She knew she couldn't bear to feel how cold they were. She still remembered the coldness of her great-grandma's skin and did not want to repeat the experience. After taking several deep breaths in the bathroom and splashing cold water on her face, Robin re-entered the visitation room and ran smack into Stephanie.

"Hi, Robin, um, will you help me put my letter in Scott's casket?" Stephanie, the girl who had hated Robin for being the recipient of Scott's attention, was now asking for a favor.

But that doesn't matter now, Robin told herself. *What would Scott want me to do? He would want me to be nice.*

"OK," Robin looked into Stephanie's downcast eyes and accepted the proffered letter.

Together they walked back over to where Scott lay, and Robin carefully put another letter into his coffin. She glanced over at Richie and noticed that someone had placed a pack of Wrigley's Winterfresh gum in with him.

He was always quick to offer everyone a piece of gum, she remembered. *Never again will he offer me a piece of gum.* She shuddered.

Robin found a spot to sit down next to her mother and was comforted by her mom's presence. Again her mother sensed Robin's need for silence. She wrapped her arm around Robin, and Robin leaned on her shoulder.

"We can stay as long as you want," her mom finally told her.

"I think I'm ready," Robin decided. "I just need to say goodbye to Becky."

Robin located her friend and was pleased with an invitation to spend Friday night at Becky's house. There was going to be a bonfire for the local young people after the funeral and a caving expedition on Sabbath. The girls agreed that both sounded like good distractions. Robin waved to Becky as she found her mother, and together they headed home.

CHAPTER 9

Grilled Cheese

Robin and her mother arrived early for the funeral on Friday. Robin realized how grateful she was that her mom was willing to take off several days of work to take her to the mourning events. Her dad had offered to take off time as well, but since he was a college professor in the midst of a new school year, Robin had encouraged him to keep to his normal schedule. The church parking lot was already full, and they had to walk quite a distance to the church from where they found a spot. Robin took one look at the two hearses waiting solemnly out front and almost bolted back to the car.

Entering the church, Robin and her mom signed the two guest books and were each handed two programs. Each boy had his own funeral program with his picture and the dates of his life on the front and his obituary on the back. The programs inside were similar, but each had different people listed to give the eulogy and to act as pallbearers.

As she walked by the open caskets to say her final goodbye, Robin noted that several other letters had been added to the ones that she had placed with her friends. The inside of the church was packed, so it took a bit of searching to find two open seats. Robin and her mom finally spotted Becky and saw that she had saved them spots near the middle of the room, and they hurried to sit down.

With soft background music playing, they waited in silence for the memorial service to begin. Scott Andrew Hayes, 1999-2015, and Richard Michael Snow, 1998-2015. As she stared at their pictures and the lines representing their lives, she mourned that their bright and promising futures had now been reduced to a dash on a piece of paper.

The service began with prayer and special music. Then came the eulogies. Richie's brother was too choked up to give his talk, so someone else read what he had written. His words told how he and Richie had been two little cowboys chasing imaginary Indians and how much he would miss his brother. One of Scott's sisters told how they had always played the game, "I love you more." She ended her talk by telling Scott she loved him more.

The pastor gave his sermonette and included short narratives that he had found on Facebook. Robin was pleased when a couple of her memories were mentioned, and she learned things about the boys that she hadn't known like how Richie had dreamed of becoming an engineer, and Scott wanted to be a computer technician. She also learned that one of the boys had recently been inquiring about attending prayer conference that year.

As she looked around the packed sanctuary and listened to the testimonies from others, she was again reminded how incredible Scott and Richie had been. Lyrics from a song she'd heard on the Christian radio station popped into her head. "A beginning and an ending, dates upon a stone. But the moment in the middle is how we will be known. 'Cause what defines us can be found within a line, finding reason for our time."

Oh, what was the name of that song? She'd heard it a few times and really liked how it emphasized the importance of the things we do every day. She discreetly typed some of the lyrics into her phone. *Oh yes! It is called "The Line Between the Two," by Mark Harris.* Her eyes scanned the tear-stained faces of most of the audience. *Richie and Scott certainly left a huge legacy behind!*

She turned her attention back to the pastor and listened attentively to the message of hope he was offering. She loved how he said that someday death would be defeated and that death itself would die. When Jesus came for the second time, she'd see her friends again.

The funeral service ended with Jeremy Camp's song, "There Will be a Day." She remembered that the song had been inspired by the artist's own loss of his wife to cancer. As the chorus washed over her, Robin yearned for the day when Jesus would come and take away all the pain and suffering this world has to offer. She clung to the words, "Troubled soul, don't lose your heart 'cause joy and peace He brings and the beauty that's in store outweighs the hurt of life's sting."

The pallbearers were now standing up to move the caskets to the waiting hearses. Richie was carried by junior and senior boys that had been his friends and Scott was carried by male church members who had watched him grow up. Fresh tears welled up in her eyes as she noticed tears in each of the pallbearers' eyes. There was something about watching a grown man cry that touched your soul deep inside.

> "Troubled soul, don't lose your heart 'cause joy and peace He brings and the beauty that's in store outweighs the hurt of life's sting."

Robin and her mother rose to join the crowd of people headed out to their cars to join the funeral procession. They soon pulled their car into the motorcade and followed the line of cars out to the gravesites. The families had chosen a small cemetery off the very road where Scott's and Richie's lives had ended. It was peaceful, serene, and beautiful. Robin thought it would be a nice place for them to wait for Jesus to come again.

During the short graveside service, Robin was reminded of another interment she had attended recently—the one for seven-year-old Libby. They'd sung the song, "My Life is in You Lord" by Joseph Garlington, and remembering the words seemed to bolster Robin's heart. Her life, hope, and strength were all in God then and would be again now.

The families again formed a receiving line, Richie's family in one row and Scott's in another, and the guests went through, again giving their condolences to the grieving parents and siblings. Robin hugged every member of each family and was especially comforted by the hug from Scott's brother, Paul. She knew Paul was taking it very hard. She'd heard he had planned on being in the car with them that night, but he had stayed at home to do homework at the last minute. She knew Paul would desperately need her prayers in the days ahead, and she determined to be a prayer warrior for him.

After the receiving line was finished, helium-filled balloons were passed around. Purple ones for Richie, green ones for Scott, and yellow ones for friendship. Each had an attached Bible verse. Robin grabbed a balloon of each color and read the Bible verses.

The purple balloon's verse contained a promise: "And God will wipe away every tear from their eyes; there shall be no more death, nor sorrow, nor crying. There shall be no more pain, for the former things have passed away" (Rev. 21:4).

The green balloon gave a directive: "Do not marvel at this; for the hour is coming in which all who are in the graves will hear His voice and come forth" (John 5:28, 29).

> "Do not marvel at this; for the hour is coming in which all who are in the graves will hear His voice and come forth"

And the yellow balloon described a remarkable scene:

> For the Lord Himself will descend from heaven with a shout, with the voice of an archangel, and with the trumpet of God. And the dead in Christ will rise first. Then we who are alive and remain shall be caught up together with them in the clouds to meet the Lord in the air. And thus we shall always be with the Lord. Therefore comfort one another with these words. (1 Thess. 4:16–18)

Each verse ended with a note saying "In loving memory of Richie Snow and Scott Hayes." Such comforting words from

God's Word. God had promised there would be more than this world had to offer, and Robin was comforted by the fact that Scott and Richie were just sleeping and would be waiting in their graves until Jesus came back to take them home.

All the days, months, and years that they sleep in their graves will only seem like seconds to them, Robin consoled herself with the thought.

With a count to three, the crowd released their balloons. Robin watched them twirl up into the air, a burst of color against the clear blue sky, until the balloons finally drifted out of sight. She hoped the verses would find their way to others who might be suffering to offer encouragement to them.

The crowd began to thin as people headed back to Sunnydale for a potluck. Robin saw people taking flowers from the beautiful arrangements draping each coffin and went over to get one from each to save. She carefully took a carnation from Richie's arrangement, but by the time she reached Scott's, all the flowers were gone. Mrs. Hayes saw that Robin was disappointed not to get one of the roses and offered one of her very own from the handful that she had taken. Robin was touched by the gesture.

Robin and her mother joined the funeral convoy back to the school. During the potluck, Robin sat with Becky and each girl drank three cups of grape soda. The rest of the afternoon passed in a blur as people continued to visit and share their memories. Finally, Robin's mother said she needed to go pick John up from school, so Robin retrieved her clothes to put in Becky's car and hugged her mother goodbye.

"I'll see you tomorrow night," her mother told her. "Be careful tomorrow!"

"I will. Bye," Robin said. She took her clothes and found Becky.

As the sun began to set, the bonfire was lit, and some of the church members and teachers from the school led out in vespers with the young people. As the fire blazed, they went around the circle, with each person telling someone else why they were thankful for him or her. It was a good reminder that a person never knows when the last chance to tell loved ones they are important will be.

After the fire had died down, Mr. Jones invited Becky and Robin to his house for grilled cheese sandwiches. Since he was their ride, Becky asked her brother if he would come back and get them later. He agreed, and the two girls walked with their science teacher over to his house. As Mr. Jones grilled sandwiches in his Panini press, he asked them how they were doing.

Robin remembered a recent news segment where a family member of someone who had just been murdered was asked the same question. He had responded with these words: "I don't know."

She hadn't comprehended at the time how someone could be at a place where they didn't know how they felt. Now she understood. Some moments she felt as if she wasn't going to be able to go on. Other moments she felt numb. The man on TV had said he was just looking for the strength that was right in front of him. That's what she was trying to do now. To just get through the next moment and then the next moment that was ahead of her.

Mr. Jones spent a few hours listening to Robin and Becky talk about their friends and their loss. The girls could not find words to express how grateful they were for his listening ear. Somehow, though, they felt he understood.

CHAPTER 10
Caving

Becky and Robin arose early on Sabbath morning and headed to meet the bus that would take them caving. Robin was pleased to see that Paul was along and tried to sit near him. His presence was comforting because he reminded her so much of his brother. Scott and Paul had shared the same facial features and eyes and at one point, Robin was almost convinced that it had all been a bad dream, and Scott was on the bus after all.

The drive to Meramec State Park in southern Missouri was a long one, and the group distracted themselves with some of the usual travel games. The teenagers played the alphabet game first, finding letters on highway signs and license plates. Robin almost won but got stuck on the letter Q because she'd missed the Dairy Queen sign the victor had spotted.

Many of the group played "Mercy," slapping each other's hands until they were quite red. Then someone suggested they sing camp songs, and they belted out their favorite praise songs at the top of their lungs. Normally the sponsors wouldn't allow the hand slapping or the loud singing, but she realized today they were making an exception. Robin felt conflicted about having any fun.

Is it a betrayal to their memory to laugh today?

When the sponsors finally suggested they play some quieter games, some of the young people played Rook and other card games. Some of the boys challenged the girls with logic puzzles. Robin knew she impressed them when she deciphered one quickly that no one else had even been able to answer. She shyly admitted that her dad had given her many analytical scenarios to solve as she was growing up, so she'd had some practice.

At one point there was a thumb war tournament. After winning a few matches, Robin was thrilled when she was able to play against Paul. His hand was warm. She hoped he didn't notice that hers was clammy.

"One, two, three, four, I declare a thumb war," Robin and Paul said in unison.

Normally when Robin played thumb war, she'd try a sneak attack with her index finger. Today she knew she needed to play fair. Paul won, but she didn't mind one bit.

When they arrived at the park, and Robin stood to exit the bus, she almost bumped her head.

"There's a roof there," Paul told her.

"Thanks!" Robin smiled at him.

The group had worship then headed to a cave that one of the leaders told them was called "Little Scott's Cave."

The name is so appropriate. Scott sure would have liked having a cave named after him, Robin noted.

As they walked through the woods, Robin noticed the boys were knocking down trees left and right. She understood their pent-up frustrations. Their friends had just died, and they could do nothing about it. When they arrived at the cave, Robin became nervous. It looked more like a hole in the ground than a cave to Robin. She was scared, but she climbed down inside with the others.

Though a novice spelunker, somehow Robin ended up with the more experienced, faster group. There were a lot of challenging areas, and Robin had to focus on what she was doing. This took her mind off the reality of the situation and her pain for a few moments at a time here and there. Then she would remember why they were there and realize how much fun Richie and Scott would be having, and her world would come crashing down again.

During one particularly challenging part, Robin voiced her concerns about falling to a nearby junior boy.

"I think you can do it," he told her. "But I'll give you a nickel if you fall." He grinned.

She laughed and for some reason that simple offer gave her the courage to continue. Later during another tricky spot, the same junior boy helped her down off a ledge. She slipped and accidentally pushed him into a rock.

She blushed bright red. "Are you OK?"

"Just a flesh wound," he joked, "I'll live." They both immediately sobered at the irony of that statement. They were there because their friends were no longer alive.

Several hours later the group, tired and really dirty, emerged out of the cave. Blinking their eyes slowly, they adjusted again to the light. Robin had bruises on her arms and knees, had hit her head multiple times (thank goodness for the helmets they had been forced to wear!), and had hit her spine hard once.

The pain feels good, she thought. *Pain means I am alive.*

The group found some showers in the park to clean up as best they could before having sundown worship and returning to the bus for the ride home. They stopped at a Taco Bell in town, and while everyone was eating, Robin overheard Angie talking to one of the adults. Robin knew Angie was taking the deaths especially hard.

> *The pain feels good,*
> **she thought.**
> *Pain means I am alive.*

"Fun on this earth just isn't worth it," Angie told the sponsor.

Robin didn't want to be caught eavesdropping so headed back to her table. *Angie is right,* she thought. *I don't want to be here on this stupid earth any longer.*

The lyrics to the chorus of Chris Tomlin's "All of Creation" song popped into her head. *Like a bride, waiting for her groom, we'll be a church, ready for You, every heart longing for our King, we sing...*

"Even so, come, Lord Jesus, come," Robin whispered. *Come and take us to heaven right now!* Robin knew that only then would her heart truly be soothed.

The ride back to Centralia was uneventful, but as they got closer, Robin began to feel sick. How would she ever survive classes on Monday?

PART THREE

A Time for Healing

*"He will swallow up death in victory;
and the Lord God will wipe away tears from all faces"*
(Isa. 25:8, KJV).

CHAPTER 11
Back to Class

Forcing herself out of bed on Monday morning, Robin reminded herself that it had now been almost a week since the accident. She wondered if her life was forever going to be divided into two parts: before and after the accident, before and after her loss. Before and after it felt like her world had ended.

She skipped breakfast and made it to Life Skills a few minutes before the bell. As she walked into the classroom, she noticed the desks had been rearranged. The reason was clear. It was supposed to be easier on her and her classmates with no empty seat as evidence of where Scott used to sit. No reminder of where he'd sat with her over in the corner section, with just him and her making up a group. The teacher announced a seating chart, and Robin quickly found her name and seat.

Chapel was no easier. Since the sophomores sat in alphabetical order for attendance, it was clear why there was an empty seat. The same for the empty seat in the juniors' section. After chapel, she headed to work, hoping for some distractions. She was doing OK until she was assigned to open the sympathy cards that were pouring in. Memories from last year when Sunnydale had sent similar cards to a sister school who had lost a student to drowning rushed into her head. Had that young man's friends felt like her? She felt like she was sinking in quicksand. Down, down, down; deep into a pit of despair.

She was supposed to go through the cards and put out the best ones for display. Robin wondered if Mrs. Hanson was torturing her or if she'd thought the sympathy notes would be good for her grieving worker. She suspected the latter, but at certain moments during the morning it felt like the former. She knew her boss was also grieving the losses, and sometimes Robin caught her tearing up while talking on the phone.

Her favorite sympathy mail included a banner that was signed by an entire sophomore class from a nearby school and two cards with encouraging quotes. In one, someone had written the line, "Sometimes when things look bleakest, we can see God clearest." Robin certainly agreed with that. God's comforting presence was the only thing holding her up at times.

The other line she really liked was the following one: "Earth has no sorrow that heaven can't heal." How true that statement was! Only heaven could truly heal the pain of losing people you loved. Heaven held the beautiful promise of being reunited with them again. How she now longed for the day that Jesus would come again!

> "*Earth* has no sorrow that heaven can't heal."

She whispered that statement over and over to herself the rest of the day—especially as she walked to lunch and saw that the flag was at half-staff, or when she noticed the purple and green ribbons on the shirts of many of her classmates. She continued to cling to the promise when, during each class that afternoon, the new seating arrangements reminded her of her loss.

Tuesday morning dawned bright and early, a week since she'd found out. She'd been naively happy as she'd typed her paper, blissfully remembering hanging out with Scott the day before. She had liked him so much, couldn't help but still like him even though he was gone. Had he liked her? It hurt that she would never know.

She knew that Richie would have been able to help her

through the loss of Scott. She also knew her close friends were worried about her, but they didn't really understand. Richie would have understood. But he was also gone, and she felt so alone.

During work on Wednesday, the principal showed Mrs. Hanson some pictures that he had taken of the car at the local junkyard. Robin told herself not to look, but she couldn't stop herself. What she saw shocked her. An indentation of the telephone pole was clearly visible on the front part of the cab of the car. The roof was crushed exactly where their heads would have been. It was obvious why neither boy had survived the crash even though she had heard they had been buckled in. Later that day she cringed as she was instructed to remove their names from the class rosters.

On Thursday she received an email from Mrs. Smith, the wife of the boys' dean. Mrs. Smith asked if Robin would like to eat lunch at the dean's apartment on Sabbath afternoon with her and Mr. Smith. She was surprised, but then she realized that Mr. and Mrs. Smith had been her faculty family parents the year before, so naturally they would be concerned about her. Each faculty member had several students that they "adopted" for the year and "family" get-togethers happened several times throughout the year where students went to staff houses for games, movies, and food.

Richie was in our faculty family, too. She wiped the tears away that had welled up, and she quickly emailed her response saying she would like that very much.

Friday passed slowly and painfully. *It's been one week since I last saw them*, Robin mused. *One week since their bodies were lowered into the ground.*

Finally, it was Sabbath. After church, Robin headed over to the boys' dean's apartment for lunch. Both Mr. and Mrs. Smith greeted her warmly with a hug.

"How are you doing?" Mrs. Smith asked carefully.

"OK," Robin admitted. "Some days are better than others."

"We hope you like lasagna," Mr. Smith had headed back to the kitchen to finish making a delicious looking green-leaf salad. Robin watched as he chopped tomatoes and cucumbers then added some shredded carrots into the mix.

"I do," Robin took an approving sniff of the aroma coming from the oven. "It smells great."

Mrs. Smith and Robin sat down at the table. Mr. Smith brought over the salad, and the timer went off for the lasagna. Robin thought it was really nice that Mr. Smith was helping with the food. She could tell that Mrs. Smith appreciated it, too.

Mr. Smith put on oven mitts and pulled the hot dish out of the oven, replacing it with a cookie sheet laden with garlic bread. "The bread will be done in a few minutes," he said. "But we can start with the salad now."

Mr. Smith joined the two girls at the table, and they bowed their heads as he said prayer. As they ate the plentiful meal, the couple slowly drew conversation from Robin. At first, the topics were safe. How were her classes going? What had she done during the summer? Then the topic drifted to the elephant in the room.

Robin admitted that she'd been at Scott's house that last Saturday night. She was surprised to learn that the Smiths already knew that. She told them how hard it had been to learn of the accident and asked how they had found out.

"It was hard for us, too!" Mrs. Smith told her.

"We found out that Monday night. We gathered together with the other deans and spent most of the night praying for Scott's family and for God to save Richie's life if it was His will," Mr. Smith added.

"How could God let this happen?" Robin lamented.

"Sweetie, we have to remember that God has given us the gift of free will. And even though sometimes it pains Him, He allows us to make our own choices. While at times it is more painful and devastating than others, there are consequences when we make bad decisions," Mrs. Smith reminded her.

> **God has given us the gift of free will. And even though sometimes it pains Him, He allows us to make our own choices.**

"But He could have prevented it!" Robin insisted.

"Yes, He could have, but we have to remember that His will is not our own. And good can come out of bad circumstances if we choose to learn from our mistakes. The best thing we can do now is to remember our friends and live like they would have wanted us to," Mrs. Smith said, looking sad.

"Remember last year in faculty family when you and Richie beat me at Blackout Bingo?" Mr. Smith changed the subject.

"Yes!" Robin laughed. "You called us punks."

"You two were in cahoots," he retorted. "I'm still not convinced you didn't cheat somehow."

"When we went to McDonald's for ice cream that one time, do you remember how Richie drank that 'surprise' shake you kids made?" Mrs. Smith chimed in.

"Yeah, it had a mixture of all the fountain drinks, salt, pepper, and even dabs of ice cream and ketchup!" Robin smiled at the memory.

"Gross!" The Smiths said in unison.

"I laughed so hard I cried. And he drank it down without a complaint." Robin knew she could not have been that brave. "I hope he didn't get sick afterward!"

They continued to reminisce about the good times they had spent with Richie and Scott. Robin was grateful for the listening ears, and as she headed back across campus that afternoon to the girls' dorm, she knew she was not alone in her sorrow.

CHAPTER 12
Depression

Two weeks after the accident, it was time to take school pictures. Robin knew that she looked tired, and the usual shine was gone from her eyes. She hadn't cared much about her appearance since she'd found out, but she managed to use concealer to hide the dark circles under her eyes. She also did her best not to cry the day before it was her turn to sit in front of the photographer's camera.

She'd cried every day since that horrible Tuesday morning. Every night she wrote in her journal counting the days they had been gone and detailing her feelings of loss. Every memory that she remembered about Richie and Scott was chronicled so that she wouldn't forget anything about them. She printed off any articles she read online about the accident for her scrapbook and wrote letters in the memory books for Richie's and Scott's families.

Later that week, the sophomore class voted for their officers. Robin had been freshman class secretary and had enjoyed the work, so she ran for several positions. She was disappointed when she lost every race.

It doesn't really matter anyway. All that matters is that my friends are gone, she told herself.

After class elections, Robin seemed to lose all interest in everything. She did her schoolwork because she wanted to get good
grades and keep her 4.0 GPA, but her classes no longer held their
usual draw. She alternated between feelings of anger towards the
two boys: for driving fast and for being out late on a school night,
and feelings of utter emptiness. She heard rumors that Richie had
gotten a large speeding ticket a few months back. Why hadn't he
learned his lesson? And if Paul stayed home to do homework, why
hadn't they stayed home to do it, too? Why couldn't it have been
someone else? Why had God allowed her friends to die?

She thought about the Bible verses in Matthew 6:19–21 that
warned people not to lay up their treasures on earth, where moths
or rust could destroy them, but to store up their treasures in
heaven. Her treasures were definitely in heaven; for that was the
only place she'd see Scott and Richie again.

One night when she was feeling especially down she wrote in
her journal: *Jesus needs to come now and take us all home. I don't
want to be on this awful earth any longer! I don't want to be old when
I see them again. I want to see them again now! I know this sounds
bad, but I wish I could die, too, so the next thing I would know is
Jesus coming again. That way I wouldn't have to deal with the huge
hole that Scott and Richie have left. They are lucky in that they are
just sleeping until Jesus comes and
don't have to deal with the trou-
bles of this world anymore. I have
always wondered if anyone would
be sad at my funeral. Would people
even miss me? I hope so. I know*
*Scott and Richie would have been proud to see how many people
loved them. Why couldn't it have been me instead? I would gladly
have taken their places.*

> *I know this sounds bad,
> but I wish I could die, too,
> so the next thing I would
> know is Jesus coming again.*

She thought about the lyrics to a song called "Mad World"
by Gary Jules. "I think it's kinda funny. I think it's kinda sad. The
dreams in which I'm dying are the best I've ever had." Death
seemed like a welcoming escape. Why couldn't she have been in
the car with them?

Robin's mournful musings were interrupted by a knock on her door. When she opened the door, she was surprised to see Samantha, another sophomore from her hall, standing there. *Samantha was the one Scott told he would pay tomorrow on the day he died. Tomorrow never came,* she thought.

"Hi Robin," Samantha said, looking a little nervous. "Aubrey and I are starting a Bible study tonight, and we wanted to know if you'd like to join."

A Bible study sounds better than sitting here in misery, Robin reasoned. Aloud she replied, "That sounds really nice. Let me grab my Bible."

Robin locked her room, and the two girls headed down the hall to Samantha's room for an encouraging hour of reading and discussing God's Word.

It seemed providential that just like with the invitation to the Bible study, whenever Robin was really down, someone would come to her room to cheer her up, or she'd get an encouraging message on Facebook or in her email to bolster her spirits. One night the dean called her downstairs during study hall. She was surprised to see her parents waiting for her in the lobby. They had brought her a warm, red and yellow, Chiefs blanket to liven up her room and give their favorite team good luck in the current NFL season.

Several other times one or both of her parents made the drive from Columbia to Centralia to visit her on school nights. Her dad would help her with her geometry because math was her most frustrating subject and with a Master's in Math, he was pretty good at it. Her mom would bring Robin some of her favorite culinary treats. She cherished their efforts, but it was still so hard to get through each day.

The first weekend of October was alumni weekend. Robin had really enjoyed it last year, and she had looked forward to several of the activities: missing classes for career day on Friday, the returning class role calls during Sabbath school, the annual singing of the hymn "With a Voice of Singing" at church, and especially the annual alumni vs. student basketball games with the Saturday night free pizza feed. She enjoyed singing the school song and cheering for her classmates who played in the basketball games, and she looked forward to when she could return as a professional and help with some of the activities, including career day. But this year she had no interest in the weekend, and the returning alumni only signified longer lines in the cafeteria and more people using up the hot water in the dorms.

Later that month, on the one-month anniversary of the accident, Mr. Jones drove Robin and Becky to the cemetery after classes. He had even been kind enough to take them to the store to buy some flowers to put on the graves before they went. When they arrived, Mr. Jones waited in his truck while the girls went to the spot. It certainly wasn't hard to find the two fresh mounds of dirt in the otherwise pristine landscaping. It was too soon for headstones, so they carefully placed their flowers by each simple grave marker and stood in silence as they contemplated the gravity of their loss.

After a few moments, they headed back to the truck. When they climbed into the cab, Mr. Jones asked if he could pray with them. The girls nodded their heads and Mr. Jones's simple prayer asked God to be with the families of the two boys and to be with all those who missed them. When they opened their eyes, tears glistened in all three pairs.

They drove back to campus in silence. Robin did her best to eat dinner that night, but she found she had no appetite. She skipped Rec and spent the time writing a poem that she dedicated to her friends. When she was finished, Robin worked on her homework before crying herself to sleep.

It's Hard to Believe

It's hard to believe it's been so long,
Since you smiled your last smile or sang your last song.
My mind is confused; I don't know what to do.
I don't understand why it had to be you.
I want to wake up! Please tell me it's not real.
Tell me to stop the pain I feel.
I miss you both so much!
You'll never know how many lives you did touch.

CHAPTER 13
Grief Group

In November, Mrs. Hanson organized a grief group for some of Richie and Scott's friends. Robin was grateful for her boss's thoughtfulness. During the first meeting, Mrs. Hanson instructed each person to draw his or her favorite memories of the boys. As she thought about what to draw, Robin scanned the rest of the group. Aaron and Angie were there as well as a few others she had heard were having a hard time with the deaths.

She finally decided on a picture of two stick figures on rides at Six Flags and a hedgehog in an anatomy skull to represent her memories of Richie. For Scott, she drew a picture of two stick figures fighting with two whale floaties and some stars depicting the Milky Way. The first meeting closed with each person explaining his or her memories as they were depicted in picture form. It was a little encouraging for Robin to know she was not alone in her continuing pain. She had thought everyone else had already moved on, but the grief group meeting indicated that this was not the case.

During the next meeting, Mrs. Hanson gave each student a handout with the five stages of grief: denial, anger, bargaining, depression, and acceptance. They read the descriptions and then they had time to talk about which stages they had been through. Robin didn't share much in the group, but later that night during study hall she re-read the handout.

As Robin thought about the stages of grief, she reflected on the ones that she had already been through. Denial when she'd first found out. Anger at them: at Richie for driving so fast; at Scott for riding with him, especially on a night when he had homework. What if he'd stayed home that night like his brother had? What if Richie had stopped driving fast after he'd gotten the huge speeding ticket? What if she'd been in the car? What if they hadn't died, would she be dating Scott or would he have broken her heart? Her heart *was* broken, and it was because of him… but he hadn't done it on purpose, so it wasn't the same. She realized she was still going through the bargaining phase. She also knew the "what if's" were driving her crazy. It wasn't fair that their lives had ended so abruptly. It wasn't fair that she would never know how Scott had felt about her. It just wasn't fair! As she read through the grief stage descriptions, she realized she was experiencing depression as well.

She knew some of her "friends" thought she was obsessing, perhaps even over-exaggerating her pain for attention. One girl had even told her, "It was a long time ago." *How can they think I am mourning for attention? How can they expect me to have gotten over it already?* She was thankful Hannah was still supportive and always listened when Robin needed to talk.

> She also knew the "what if's" were driving her crazy.

Robin opened up her computer and typed in the URL for the Family Life Radio (FLR) website and began streaming its music in the background. She had started listening to the Christian radio station recently because of the encouraging stories and uplifting music. She couldn't bear to listen to any of the popular radio stations right now because all the love songs they played made her stomach upset.

She'd heard stories from others on FLR that they seemed to play just the right song at exactly the right moment. She hadn't experienced that yet, but she hoped that it might be the case for

her today. As she worked on her homework, she hummed the lyrics to the songs that she already knew.

Suddenly, a song started playing that stopped her in her tracks.
"It's time for letting go, all of our 'if onlys' 'cause we don't have
a time machine. And even if we did, would we really want to use
it? Would we really want to go change everything?" She googled
those lines and found that the song was called "Miracle of the
Moment" by Steven Curtis Chapman.

As she listened, the words seemed like a balm to her wounded
soul. What if she could go back in time? Would she go back and try
and convince Richie not to drive so fast? Logic told her the hubris
of youth had made him think he was invincible, and he probably
wouldn't have listened. So if she couldn't stop the accident, would
she want to go back in time and never meet them? No, she was a better person because she had known them, and the time she had gotten to spend with Scott and Richie would always be precious to her.

Would she have told Scott how she had felt about him? Sure, it
would have been nice to know if he had returned the feelings, but
what if he hadn't? Would that only make things harder? Or worse,
what if he had, and she'd always wonder what could have been.
No, maybe not knowing if he had liked her back was better. Would
she go back in time and try and be in the car with them? She had
told herself many times lately that no one would miss her if she
were gone. But she knew better. Her mom, dad, and even John
would miss her very much. And so would her friends: Hannah and
Becky; and now Aubrey and Samantha from Bible study. They had
all made it clear that she was important to them. So, no, she didn't
really wish she had been in the car.

The chorus seemed to reach in and touch her heart: "So
breathe it in and breathe it out, and listen to your heartbeat.
There's a wonder in the here and now. It's right there in front of
you, and I don't want you to miss the miracle of the moment. And
if it brings you tears...."

Robin realized she was crying. "Then taste them as they fall.
Let them soften your heart."

Robin did as the song suggested and licked some of the salty liquid running down her cheeks. "And if it brings you laughter, then throw your head back, and let it go...."

Wow, God, this message seems to be just for me! Robin continued to listen in awe to the rest of the song, convinced the song choice had been God-led to comfort her. She didn't get any more studying done that night. Instead, she spent the rest of the evening in Bible study and prayer.

> *Robin continued to listen in awe to the rest of the song, convinced the song choice had been God-led to comfort her.*

Right before Thanksgiving home leave, Robin decided to move into Hannah's room. She was finding her own room quite lonely lately, and she spent most of her time there anyway. The girls bunked their beds with Robin getting the top bunk. Hanging blankets down over the edge, Hannah was thrilled to get a little sleeping cave.

Thanksgiving vacation passed in a blur. Normally Robin loved spending the holiday at her grandmother's house—stuffing her face with delicious food and stopping only when she was too full to eat anymore. Her dad always joked on Thanksgiving (and at buffets) that he got so full that he became afraid of bumping into sharp objects for fear his stomach would burst.

Robin's mom was the youngest of six children, so her grandparents' house was usually full of forty or more people ranging in age from those needing diapers to those with graying (or missing) hair. Laughter and friendly arguments, sometimes even on taboo group topics like politics or religion, were heard in every room of the house, and there was always a game of catch with the football in the front or backyard. Card games with her many cousins were always fun, and games like Pit could turn quite competitive. But this year nothing seemed to excite Robin, and she was all too happy to head home early after the big family dinner.

After break, Robin's mom drove her back to campus and stayed for a while to help her and Hannah decorate for Christmas. They put wrapping paper on their door, and her mom gave them each an ornament with their names on it to top off the festive look. They also strung icicle lights all over, held up by thumb tacks pushed into the wall. The year before Robin had learned that duct tape didn't hold the lights up very well, but thumb tacks did. The tiny holes could later be easily filled with toothpaste. She wasn't sure if that was legal or not but she hadn't gotten into trouble yet.

Every night Robin and Hannah would stay up late having worship and praying together. Even after lights out, the glow from the icicle lights gave plenty of illumination for their Bibles. One night after lights out, they were surprised by a knock on the door.

Hannah got out of bed and answered the door. The girls' dean stood there with a serious expression on her face. "I've been watching your room for the last few nights," she said, "and I've noticed that you've been keeping your Christmas lights on way past curfew. What are you up to?"

"We're sorry," Hannah said. "We're having worship."

"We're almost finished, and we'll try not to stay up too late again," Robin added.

Clearly surprised at the reason for their non-compliance, the dean backtracked a little. "No, it's OK if you stay up for worship," she said. "Do try to get into bed on time." She walked away, heading back down the hall.

Hannah closed the door, and the two girls burst into giggles as they pictured their prim and proper dean standing outside the dorm to see who still had their lights on. They finished worship with a prayer and went to bed.

Mrs. Hayes invited Scott's former friends to her house for a celebration of what would have been his sixteenth birthday on the sixteenth of December. *He's missing his golden year,* Robin mused as she looked at the invitation. And then she remembered that Richie would have been eighteen on the eighteenth of April, so he was going to miss his golden year as well.

The weekend before Christmas vacation, a small group gathered at the Hayes household to watch movies and celebrate Scott's life. It felt wrong to be back in the loft without Scott and Richie, and the familiar painful feeling squeezed at Robin's heart, robbing her of any joy she might have found. When it was time to go,

Mrs. Hayes thanked each person for coming and told them she didn't want them to be strangers. But Robin knew she wouldn't be ready to come back for a long time.

Robin studied hard for her finals and soon she was headed home for the almost three weeks of Christmas break. She looked forward to the time with her family, away from the constant reminders of Scott and Richie at school.

Robin had a dental appointment to tighten her braces over break. Instead of her usual inconspicuous silver rubber bands, she chose purple and green bands in honor of Scott and Richie. She was both happy and sad each time she looked in the mirror and was reminded of her friends.

Will I ever be able to look at purple, my own favorite color, again without thinking of Richie?

CHAPTER 14

The CROWs

During Christmas break, Mrs. Snow contacted Robin to see if she wanted to have any of Richie's things. Robin was honored to be remembered by his mother as one of his friends, and she promptly asked her mom to drive her up to Centralia to meet with Mrs. Snow. Robin came home that afternoon with a baseball hat and a purple-and-silver athletic jersey. Each of the items seemed to embody Richie's active spirit, and Robin knew she would treasure the gifts. But looking at them only made her sad, and she had to put them away for now.

Will the ache in my heart ever go away?

Robin was surprised at how fast the rest of break flew by and before she knew it, she was celebrating the beginning of a new year with the local church youth group. She tried to be as carefree as the other young adults but just couldn't muster up her usual festive spirit. Cora had brought Jack to the party, and as Robin watched them together, she couldn't help but think about her missing friends.

It sure would have been nice to ring in the new year with Scott, she told herself.

Back at school, Robin was pleased to learn that Samantha and Aubrey wished to continue their weekly Bible studies. She had enjoyed hanging out with Cora over break (when Jack wasn't around, of course), so she invited her to join their group.

In their grief group, Mrs. Hanson helped the members make two crosses to put on the telephone pole at the scene of the accident. After they'd placed the crosses where they thought looked best and carefully nailed them into place, they stood together and sang the hymn "Because He Lives." Though the late-January wind was cold, Robin's heart was warmed by the words of the song: "Because He lives, I can face tomorrow. Because He lives, all fear is gone."

Is it true? Because Jesus lives, is everything really going to be OK? She wasn't sure that life could ever be truly OK again, but the words gave her the bit of hope she'd been missing over the past four months.

"*Because* He lives, I can face tomorrow. Because He lives, all fear is gone."

Mrs. Hanson and the rest of the grief group were disappointed to learn that their crosses disappeared that very week. They had gotten permission from the telephone company, so what was the problem? They decided to try again, and this time gathered together to put two beautiful wreaths, one garnished with purple ribbon and one with green ribbon, onto the pole. Again the group was devastated to learn that the wreaths disappeared soon after they were placed. After much discussion they realized the symbols must be too painful of a reminder to someone, so they decided to give up. The group knew all too well that grief could cut deep into a person's very soul, and they had no desire to inflict additional pain on anyone.

The week before Valentine's Day, Samantha got a bright idea during their Bible study.

"What if we make Valentine's cards for everyone in the school?" she asked. "That way we'll know that everyone gets at least one card and knows someone is thinking about him or her."

"That's a great idea!" Aubrey agreed.

"Why don't we come up with some kind of code name to sign them with?" Cora chimed in.

"Let's see if we can come up with an acronym of our names to use," Robin said. She couldn't help but catch onto the excitement of her friends. "Let's see, Cora Whitman, Samantha Oliver, Aubrey Riley, and Robin Carter ... what word can we make with C, S, A, and R?"

"CARS!" Aubrey suggested, and they all laughed.

"We can come up with something better," Samantha insisted.

"What about using our last names?" Cora proposed as another solution.

"W, O, R, and C," Robin mused over the letters on a piece of scratch paper.

"WORC doesn't sound very fun," Aubrey noted as she looked over Robin's shoulder.

Suddenly the letters clicked, and Robin squealed, "I've got it! How about the CROWs?"

The other girls agreed it was a perfect *non de plume*, and they officially became the CROWs. They quickly set to work finding paper and other supplies to start making their Valentine's Day cards, signing each card: "Love, the Crows."

Even though they worked tirelessly on the cards during their free time that week, they wanted to keep their identities classified and soon realized they didn't have much "private" spare time. Plus, there *were* more than 150 students at the school. They each breathed a sigh of relief as they finished up their last card. The deans were happy to pass out the cards and keep their secret safe. During their next Bible study, the girls all agreed that it was especially fun doing something nice for someone when the random act of kindness was undercover.

Later that month, a representative from UNOS, the United Network for Organ Sharing, came to tell the student body about the benefits of signing up to be an organ donor. Robin knew that some students had been upset to learn that Richie's organs had been donated. Now hearing that several people's lives had been saved from his organs, Robin realized that she'd like to be an organ donor someday.

On the first Sabbath of spring break, Robin and her family went to Stephens Lake Park in Columbia for a nice Sabbath afternoon walk. The pretty flowers around the path and the warm sunshine indicated that spring had finally won its annual tug-of-war with winter. Turtles and fish were abundant, but it was the migrating geese that caught Robin's eye. Well, one Canada Goose, in particular.

Robin had been afraid of Canada Geese since she was little. Her dad had tried to raise some for her grandparents' pond. He had warned Robin and John not to take the birds out of their cage without supervision. But like most children, being told not to do something is irresistible. One day, Robin and John were naughty and snuck the two birds, which at the time were nearly their size, out of the cage and down to the creek behind their house. When it was time to go back inside, the birds had refused, threatening to attack the children with their beaks until they finally swam away downstream and out of sight.

Today at Stephens Lake, Robin was no longer afraid of geese. However, as she sat on a bench and waited while her family finished walking around the lake, she did feel very sorry for one. Unlike its buddies, one goose was missing the top of its beak. She couldn't help but watch it for a while as it tried to glean for food. She noticed that the other geese picked on it as well. Had it been hit by a car? Or had some necrotizing bacteria (like what they'd read about in Biology) taken its toll on the appendage? Watching the large bird struggle to survive broke Robin's heart. But then she realized that it must be breaking God's heart even more. He was the Creator of the goose after all.

There was a verse somewhere in Matthew that talked about how God knew when each sparrow fell. She opened the Bible application on her phone and searched for the text.

"There it is!" She hadn't meant to say it aloud and silently began to read.

"Are not two sparrows sold for a copper coin? And not one of them falls to the ground apart from your Father's will. But the very hairs on your head are all numbered. Do not fear therefore; you are of more value than many sparrows" (Matt. 10:29–31).

Wow, she thought. *All these months I have been wallowing in my own pain and neglecting to remember that the King of the Universe loved Richie and Scott more than anyone on Earth did.*

Robin remembered a text they had read during a recent Bible study, 1 John 4:8, which stated that God is love. She then thought about the wondrous message of John 3:16. *God sent His own Son to die for Richie, for Scott. Even for me!*

She searched through the music on her phone until she found the song "One Thing Remains" by Jesus Culture.

She found herself whispering the lyrics, "Higher than the mountains that I face, stronger than the power of the grave, constant through the trial and the change, one thing remains.... Your love never fails. It never gives up. It never runs out on me."

A sense of peace seemed to fill Robin as she sat waiting for her family, listening to music while watching the beautiful and graceful birds that God had made and contemplating His endless love for her and the rest of humanity.

Later that day, Robin wrote this poem:

I Ask Why?
I open my eyes
In this world full of lies,
Where everything dies,
And I ask why?

I see little kids with nothing to eat.
I hear that wives are being beat.
I know animals are killed for their meat,
And I ask why?

This world is a terrible place
Flung way out into space.
Life seems like such a waste,
And I ask why?

Why? Because of the presence of sin.
Why? Because of a choice made way back then.

Why then did this world even begin?
And I ask why?

Why? Because Jesus loves me.
Enough to die to set me free.
He hung for me upon that tree,
I no longer have to ask why.

CHAPTER 15

The Lord's Prayer

The yearbooks arrived in late April, and students frantically passed them around, asking their friends and teachers for signatures and personalized messages. Of course, the year was dedicated to Richie and Scott, and while it hurt to look at their pictures, Robin was pleased to see they had used one of the pictures she and Becky had taken of Scott. Her favorite, the one where he'd been looking at her and slightly away from the camera was front and center of the dedication page.

Robin and her friends continued to have their Bible study as the school year came to an end. During their last meeting, as they were reading Matthew 6, something clicked inside Robin's head as they read verses 9 and 10: "In this manner, therefore, pray: Our Father in heaven, hallowed by Your name. Your kingdom come. Your will be done on earth as it is in heaven."

"The Lord's Prayer asks for God's will to be done on Earth as it is in heaven. That's because His will isn't being done here!"

"The Lord's Prayer asks for God's will to be done on Earth as it is in heaven. That's because

His will isn't being done here!" Robin exclaimed. "God didn't choose for them to die; Richie and Scott died because of sin," she added.

Cora, Samantha, and Aubrey agreed, and they began a lively discussion of why God allowed bad things to happen to good people. He allowed people to have free will, and He couldn't stop the consequences of bad choices. The sinful nature of the world is what caused terrible things to happen, not God.

"I watched a sermon by Mark Finley on 3ABN or the Hope Channel; I can't remember which," Cora started. "He made the point of asking what takes more faith: seeing a loved one healed of cancer or watching them die and still praising God for His goodness?"

"And look at Job," Aubrey said. "He suffered all kinds of tragedies and still praised God."

"I heard a quote by Lee Strobel that said, 'Only in a world where faith is difficult can faith exist,'" Samantha contributed.

"Isn't he that Christian apologist who used to live in Columbia?" Robin asked.

"Yes, he was a former atheist and worked at the Tribune!" Samantha exclaimed.

Robin and Samantha talked for a few minutes about a book of Strobel's that both girls had read and then Aubrey and Cora brought the conversation back to the Bible study's topic of why bad things happened to good people.

"There are a lot of Christian songs that address this topic. Maybe we can look at the words of one of them as we finish today's study?" Cora suggested.

"Good idea!" Aubrey agreed. "I really like 'This is My Father's World.'"

The girls googled the hymn and many hits came up. They choose the Wikipedia link so they could also read about the song's history. Aubrey read the words to one of the earliest published versions aloud: "This is my Father's world. O let me ne'er forget that though the wrong seems oft so strong, God is the ruler yet. This is my Father's world: the battle is not done: Jesus who

> "*This* is my Father's world.
> O let me ne'er forget that though
> the wrong seems oft so strong,
> God is the ruler yet . . . "

died shall be satisfied, and earth and Heav'n be one." The words of the hymn and the Bible verses were a balm to Robin's wounded soul, and when she headed back to her room that night, she couldn't wait to tell Hannah what she'd learned. She knew there would still be many rough days ahead and that she'd never truly get over the loss of her friends. But she also knew that even though she should look forward to seeing her friends again someday in heaven, she had to accept the loss and to move on with her life. That's what Scott and Richie would want her to do.

That night during study hall, Robin was inspired to write another poem:

Time Passes
There was a day when everything seemed clear.
I lived each day with anticipation, never any fear.
I had lots of friends, my life seemed so great,
I had no idea what might be my fate.
So time passes, days go by,
An accident happens, and I wonder why.
My life is turned upside down,
I try to smile, but all I can do is frown.
And time passes, days goes by.
I still feel an ache, part of me is gone,
But I finally realize that life must go on.
Little things remind me of them so much,
Yet all I can do is remember and trust
That one day, time will pass and days will go by,
But nothing will grow old; nothing will die.
Until that day I will smile and wait,
And someday I'll make it and enter that Gate.

EPILOGUE
One Year Later

Robin woke up a few minutes before her alarm and for a moment she didn't realize the significance of the calendar's date. As the clock started to beep and she rolled over to hit snooze, the cold realization hit her and she sat up quickly, tears blurring her eyes.

She'd been doing a lot better, but during the last week, with the anniversary of the deaths drawing near, she felt that she had taken a step back in her grieving process. A year later, there were still many days when she missed Scott and Richie so badly that it hurt. She knew today would be one of those days.

She'd asked Mr. Jones if he would take her to the cemetery this afternoon after work, and he'd been kind enough to agree. She still had a long day to suffer through, though. As a junior, this year she had classes each morning and would work a few hours each afternoon. Today, as soon as she finished work, she would find Mr. Jones in his office so they could leave.

Grabbing a tissue to blow her nose, she wiped her eyes and grabbed her shower caddy to head to the bathroom to rinse off and wake up. Since she hadn't hit snooze, she had time to eat breakfast before her 6:50 a.m. class.

Even though she made her favorite toast: with butter and honey and cinnamon sprinkled on top, her breakfast tasted funny and made her sick to her stomach. She didn't eat much before she dumped her leftovers into the trash and put her tray on the moving platform that would take her used plate and cutlery to the dish room. She stared aimlessly at the tray for a bit before heading out the door to go back to the dorm and grab her backpack and head to her first class, Computer Applications.

During class, she couldn't help but think about how good Scott had been at fixing computers and how he'd dreamed of working with them someday. After class, she headed to chapel, and as she slumped down into her assigned seat in the juniors' section, she couldn't help but look at the spot in the sophomore section that Scott had once occupied. And she was sitting in the same section where Richie had last sat! At least she wasn't sitting in the same spot.

During English, she remembered throwing the koosh ball back and forth with Scott and during Algebra II she couldn't help but think of their old geometry assignment where she'd shared her crayons with him to illustrate their bulletin board shapes. Bible and Chemistry were just as hard, as she remembered fun times with Scott and Richie. When the final bell rang, she realized it had been a while since she had been so grateful to be done with classes for the day. For so long now, school had been her solitude, something she could throw herself into; her grades were something she could control.

Unlike life and death, she reminded herself.

Lunch was just as unpalatable as breakfast, but she choked some down anyway, and she made sure to drink some grape soda. Her friends tried to draw her into conversation, but she remained aloof. The most frustrating part was that no one else seemed to be suffering, and everyone else was acting like it was just like another regular day.

> *For* so long now, school had been her solitude, something she could throw herself into; her grades were something she could control.
> *Unlike life and death,* she reminded herself.

She wanted to scream at them, "Don't you know what today is? Scott and Richie are still gone!" *Can anyone even see my pain?* She wondered silently as she kept her screams and other thoughts to herself.

She left the cafeteria and headed up the stairs of the Ad building to work; she was working for Mrs. Hanson again this year. She loved her job and spent most days in comfortable conversation with her boss. Fortunately, today Mrs. Hanson seemed to sense her mood and understood her need to be silent. Mrs. Hanson also wisely kept Robin extra busy answering the main phone, transferring calls and doing office tasks. Before long, it was 4:00 p.m., and Robin was clocking out.

Mr. Jones was also quiet as he drove Robin to the cemetery. He seemed to sense her need to get lost in her thoughts. He parked a respectful distance away and waited patiently by his truck, as she walked to the section that had become so special to her. She noticed that the earth had evened out and grass had replaced the no longer visible mounds. Beautiful granite tombstones had replaced the simple markers and loving words from their families immortalized each of her friends.

She placed pretty flowers on each grave site, reflecting on the past year. A year ago, she'd woken up with so much anticipation for the day to come. So many days since then had just been something to endure. Time had eased the pain a little, but she still thought of Scott and Richie often. And sometimes when she closed her eyes, it still felt like yesterday.

And yet, a year had already passed. Even though she was now old enough to get her own driver's license, driving held no appeal for her. She just didn't have much desire to drive, and since she wasn't home very much anyway, she hadn't had very many opportunities to learn. Since she'd celebrated her sixteenth birthday the month before, she was now older than Scott had been when he died. It was just another milestone that she would reach, and he would not. It was still awhile before she'd pass Richie in age, but she knew that in time that would happen as well.

She began to pray for their families, and she thanked her

Heavenly Father for the love He had shown her over the past year. She acknowledged that He had loved them so much more than she ever could have. As she prayed, a divine peace came over her, and she knew that, though she would never completely get over them, she would never want to forget them (even if she had that choice). She was a better person because she had known them. They had taught her to treat people kindly and to find the good in everything.

As she stood in the little country cemetery, noticing the beautiful blue September sky and the slight breeze blowing through the leaves on the trees, Robin realized that the best way she could honor their lives was by living hers to the fullest, just like Richie and Scott had done and would have continued to do if they had had the chance. She took a last look at the familiar names etched in stone, took a deep breath, and headed back to her waiting teacher, her friend.

Later that night, as Robin read her evening devotional, once again the words seemed meant just for her. The chaplain had suggested she read *Ministry of Healing* by Ellen G. White, so she opened it up to where she'd left off.

Nothing is apparently more helpless, yet really more invincible, than the soul that feels its nothingness and relies wholly on the merits of the Saviour. By prayer, by the study of His word, by faith in His abiding presence, the weakest of human beings may live in contact with the living Christ, and He will hold them by a hand that will never let go. (p. 182)

The tears rolled quietly down Robin's cheeks. She had certainly felt at her weakest this past year. She'd only made it through the darkest days by clinging to the promises in

> *By* prayer, by the study of His word, by faith in His abiding presence, the weakest of human beings may live in contact with the living Christ, and He will hold them by a hand that will never let go.

God's Word. She opened her Bible to one assurance in 2 Corinthians 12:9: "And He said to me, 'My grace is sufficient for you, for My strength is made perfect in weakness.' Therefore most gladly I will rather boast in my infirmities, that the power of Christ may rest upon me."

Robin picked up her journal, opened it, and began to write. *It seems that this past year I have placed Scott and Richie on a pedestal. I told myself over and over that life would be perfect if they hadn't died and that I can't be happy now because my friends are gone. I now know deep in my heart that God's plan of salvation is much bigger than the plans I have for my life. It certainly wasn't God's will for them to die so young, but through His grace and mercy, even though their lives were cut short, they made an impact on the world. God can bring the best out of any story. He can pick up the broken pieces and transform them into something good, though it may take us years or even heaven to see.*

Maybe their legacy was kindness. I know that some positive things have already come from the ashes of this tragedy. I heard that some people quit smoking and others quit drinking. Still others realized their need to choose God now because the accident showed us that tomorrow is not guaranteed. The boys certainly made a difference in my life and perhaps I can now do the same for others.

> *God can bring the best out of any story. He can pick up the broken pieces and transform them into something good, though it may take us years or even heaven to see.*

As she closed her journal, she prayed the simple prayer written on the cover: "God grant me the serenity to accept the things I cannot change, courage to change the things I can, and the wisdom to know the difference" (Reinhold Niebuhr).

She turned on her computer and opened Family Life Radio to stream in the background as she worked on her homework. One song caught her attention. She realized it was by Phil Wickham and quickly googled some of the lyrics to find the song title.

"When My Heart is Torn Asunder," Robin read aloud. "That's definitely how I feel."

The chorus played softly in the background: "There is hope beyond the suffering, joy beyond the tears, peace in every tragedy, love that conquers fear. I have found redemption in the blood of Christ." It had been several months since she had done any creative writing, but that night Robin wrote a poem about life and what she'd learned from the death of her friends. It was a little cheesy, but it expressed her feelings and what she felt she needed to do with her life from this point on.

Changes
Life is always changing,
It never stays the same.
It doesn't matter what you do,
You'll never change the game.
Friends will die or move away,
You can hardly blink an eye.
Life leaves you without a say
And it leaves you asking why.
All that we can ever hope to do
Is take each change and grow.
You can't expect the future,
What tomorrow brings you do not know.
Live each day like it is your last.
Do what you've dreamed to do.
Make a difference in another's life,
And people will always remember you.

After she had typed and re-typed the lines of her poem to her satisfaction, she decided to read through the poem one more time. As she read, the song "Goodbye Ordinary" by Mercy Me came on the radio. The chorus spoke directly to her heart: "Live like there's no tomorrow, love extravagantly, lead a life to be followed. Goodbye ordinary."

She closed the top of her computer, grabbed a snack and went down the hall to find one of the other CROWs. It was time to accept the "new normal" and to stop wallowing in her grief. Instead of being sad, it was time to write some encouraging notes to others who were struggling.

Questions for Discussion

1. Have you ever lost a loved one? If so, how did you feel when you found out?

2. What were some of the things people did or said that helped you?

3. What were some of the things people did or said that did not help you?

4. What steps of the grieving process did you go through?

5. What did you find helpful about Robin's grieving process?

6. What, if anything, about her process did you find unhelpful or confusing?

7. What can you do for someone you love if he or she is grieving?

8. Why do you think God allows bad things to happen to good people?

9. Do those bad things happening mean God doesn't love us?

10. What promises in the Bible do you cling to as we wait for Jesus to return to take us home?

Author's Note

"I thought I could describe a state; make a map of sorrow. Sorrow, however, turns out to be not a state but a process" (C.S. Lewis, A Grief Observed).

I have been privileged to teach in the Biology/Allied Health department at Southern Adventist University since 2011. Early in 2015, we lost two young people and a retired faculty member from our school family. In the past year and a half, several other Adventist universities have faced tragedy as well, losing their students to car accidents, bicycle accidents, and even some "natural" causes. (How natural is the death of a young person?) Because of incidents like these, I have found myself talking to students about loss. One of my lab assistants told me that he didn't know how to deal with a suicide death, but that he would try and be more careful with his interactions with others. He said he always wants to be uplifting and not to bring others down because you never know what people are experiencing. A close friend of a girl who had died said she'd never experienced loss before and didn't know what to do.

I starting writing this book after the death of retired SAU professor, Dr. Ray Hefferlin (known as "Doc" to many who knew him). Although I didn't know him well, he made an impression on my life, and I know he made a profound impact on the lives of all those he met. He was so humble and down to earth that it wasn't until after his death that I learned that he was one of the smartest people I will ever meet. It was through seeing some of my students react to his death and to the deaths of the two young people in close succession that inspired me to tell this story.

When Sparrows Fall is a fictionalized account of my personal experience when I was fifteen years old. During my sophomore year in academy, I lost my two best male friends, Matthew Richard Gray and Trevor Scott Van Kort, in a tragic car accident. I went through a period of intense loneliness and depression before God finally helped me to accept their deaths and heal. When I was going through my loss, I could have used a book like this to help me deal with my feelings. Soon after the accident it seemed like the world had moved on, but I had not. It would have been nice to know that I was not alone in my pain and that it was OK to be sad and to miss my friends. The places depicted in the story are real but, while the characters are based on real people, some incidents did not happen the way they are portrayed in the book. To contemporize the story, it is now a mixture of then and now.

Years later in a college psychology class, I read a book by Michael J. Bradley called *Yes, Your Teen is Crazy!* The message of the book really hit home because it described what I already knew: for a teenager, every small thing seems like a crisis so when something like that happens, it is life-altering. Writing this book has been both painful and fulfilling. It's hard to remember what happened, but it's nice to see how God has worked in my life and the lives of others since then, helping me to look for good in the bad and to learn from the experience.

Like Robin, I was introduced to the typical stages of grief. It is important to remember that not everyone goes through every stage or stays in each stage for the same amount of time, and there is no right way to grieve. However, there are ways that can hurt us or others, so if you are struggling with loss or depression, it is OK to ask for help and to tell someone that you trust about your struggles. You are not alone and things can get better if you allow God to heal you.

Recently I read an online article from the New York Times opinion section called "Getting Grief Right." The author, Patrick O'Malley, is a psychotherapist in Fort Worth. Basically, the article emphasized how it's OK for people to work through grief on their own time tables. He suggested that grief comes in three chapters. Chapter 1 has to do with the attachment to the person who has died and the strength of the bond. He tells his patients "the size of their grief corresponds to the depth of their love." Chapter 2 is the loss itself. People often question their sanity with a great loss and begin to shut down. He said this is especially true when death is premature and traumatic. (I'll agree it may be easier to accept the death of someone who has lived a full life, but when is death not traumatic?) Chapter 3 is the long road that begins "after the last casserole dish is picked up." It's the process of healing after the world stops grieving with you.

Because of this article, I decided to divide my story up into three main parts: "A Time for Laughter," "A Time for Tears," and "A Time for Healing." The first part helps develop the bond Robin had with Scott and Richie; the second part deals with the shock and pain of the accident; the last part begins the long road to healing. I say healing and not recovery because you never really get over losing someone you love. You already know this if you've experienced any kind of big loss. If you haven't experienced this kind of pain yet, count yourself very lucky for now. Unfortunately, unless you are a hermit, you will understand someday. On earth the only guarantee we have is death. So although time eases the pain of a loss, only heaven can take it all away.

Since this story is a mixture of events that really happened and others I think will make the story more relevant and helpful, I would like to give some background on some of the things I added. My paternal grandfather died while I was a student missionary for a year in Kenya, and I'll never forget how the students and other staff at my school gave me support, whether it was a listening ear or a bunch of grapes (a huge luxury where we were!). I wrote about the homesickness that his death brought on in my first book, *It's Worth the Sacrifice*.

When I was getting my master's at Loma Linda, I had a weekly Bible study with three other girls who attended Union College with me. These studies really deepened our friendships and encouraged me in my spiritual journey. One of the girls, Rilla Vergara, led the topic about why bad things happen to good people. Her thoughts inspired me, and the Lord's Prayer example really struck home.

While in graduate school, I also had the chance to meet one of my favorite Christian apologetics' heroes, Lee Strobel. I was introduced to Strobel's work during my freshman year of college while attending a non-SDA school. My General Chemistry teacher, James "Tiger" Gordon, was a believer and even though he didn't force his beliefs on us, every now and then he would mention evidence of Creation in his lectures. He told me about Strobel's book, *A Case for Faith*, so when Strobel came and did one of the talks during Loma Linda University's Centennial Celebration, I snuck out of the service a few minutes early to get into the book signing line. When I told him I was from Columbia, MO, he took a few minutes to chat with me about the town. Even though there were many people waiting in line behind me, he took the time to make me feel special.

Many people have told me that music is an important part of their grieving process, so I have included a few songs that were meaningful to me back then, but most are ones that are more recognizable now. Last March, at the funeral of Dr. Ray Hefferlin, we sang his favorite hymn, "This is My Father's World." The song was sung with much enthusiasm by the packed church of people who came to honor him. I know he would have appreciated the beautiful sound of the music and beautiful words praising our awesome God.

Some songs and Bible texts were suggested by my supporters, and others came from the radio or sermons, Bible studies, and conversations I've had since the accident. In the last few months, a church service and a former teacher, Kelly Harden, drew my attention to hymn 477 in the SDA Hymnal, "Come Ye Disconsolate," which has the phrase, "Earth has no sorrow that heaven cannot heal." In all the years since reading that sympathy note mentioned in the book, I never knew about this song, and I find it providential that I learned about it while writing this book.

Just like it's hard to know what to do and how to feel when you are grieving, it's hard to know how to be there for someone else when they are going through a loss. Two family members were kind enough to read my manuscript and give me feedback.

Richie's brother had this to say: "Grief is intensely personal, and we have no idea how deeply it is impacting others most of the time. Just because we don't know or understand doesn't mean the process of others is any less valid. Isolation is one of the Devil's favorite tools, and he particularly delights in using it on the grieving. Ironically, when we feel so acutely the loss of loved ones, we will often suffer more by bearing our grief alone."

Scott's mother said, "That September night when the police came to my door is forever etched into my mind. I push at it and probe it to go away, but it hangs in the back of my mind like the bad memory it is. The pain has lessened through the years, but is always there. The book brought back some of those memories, but in a good way. There are places in your story when I cried and places I laughed. Seeing my son through his friends' eyes was something I never gave much thought to. He had many friends, and at the time, I knew they were grieving, too; however, I never thought that after all these years he is still remembered like he is. As his mother, that is a very special gift to me. This story, through your eyes as you lived it, will fill a gap for many adolescents going through the loss of a dear friend. The teen years can be difficult to maneuver and losing a close friend, or even just someone in their school, comes with emotions that are often hard to sort out and walk through. I truly feel your book needs to be available for adolescents to help them understand their feelings of grief and loss and to know there are brighter days ahead."

Be present for those who are grieving, but be careful. In my grief, people said things to me with the intent to make things better but sometimes were hurtful and made it worse. Make sure you are sensitive to your loved ones and don't make the situation worse. Recently, I saw a Facebook post by a woman whose husband's cancer was being treated with chemotherapy. She asked people to stop giving unsolicited advice and to stop telling her that the chemo was killing her husband. They obviously meant well but were hurting her.

An online Op-Ed article in the LA Times by Susan Silk and Barry Goldman gives advice about how to not say the wrong thing to someone who is hurting. The article suggests you draw a circle and put the name of the person who is grieving or hurting the most inside. Then you draw several concentric circles around the first one, writing the name of the person closest to that person in the next larger circle. Continue adding people progressively in larger circles based on their relationship with the person in the innermost circle.

The rules are that the person in the center can say anything they want to anyone they want. Others in bigger circles can say anything they want to people in more outer circles but must be encouraging to those in more inner circles. Essentially, you can only bring comfort to those in smaller circles than yours and can only complain to people in larger circles than yours. The article reminds the reader that everyone will get their turn in the innermost circle, so it is important to treat others like you want them to treat you when it's your turn.

Writing a book is obviously a lot of work, and I couldn't have done it without the help of my family and friends. I want to thank my husband for always listening to my big ideas and for being my best friend. My family (with special thanks to Rosalee and Sheri Dye; Ken and Pam Lee; Ann, Eric, Mary Margaret, and Sean Robinette) has always been supportive of my writing, and I'm grateful for their encouragement and suggestions. Thank you to my four students who read my early drafts, brainstorming with me, and giving me feedback as I finished writing: Hannah Kelsey (SAA class of 2014), Chantal Larsen (SAA class of 2014), Katelyn Pauls, and Molly Theus. They helped me make the story more generationally relevant and gave me invaluable advice on how to make the story better. Also, thank you to those who read part or all of the full manuscript, helping me fine tune it and for giving me suggestions on what to add and what to leave out: Andrew Gray, Sharon Harrelson, LeClare Litchfield, Renita Moore, Adrianna Panjaitan, Dina Pinette, Ciara Saranto, Cherie Smith, Stacy Stocks, Calle Turk, Lorretta Van Kort, Lisa Venteicher, and Kristie Wilder. I am also extremely grateful to everyone who believed in the project enough to make a pre-order. Without you this project would literally not have been possible. I am humbled by the generosity of my high school English teacher and friend, Kelly Harden (who proofread the manuscript draft), and my college friend, Gary Manly (who painted the beautiful cover art). And, of course, a big thank you to the team at TEACH Services, especially to my editor Avery Botticelli (a former student of mine!), and to my author advisor Carole Huddleston, who worked with me helping me to think outside of the box, answering my endless questions, and supporting me all along the way.

Just like in the story, Trevor and Matthew were just fifteen and seventeen years old when they died. They've now been gone longer than Trevor was here on this earth. And soon it will be the same for Matthew. And nothing I can do can change that. That is what's so hard about death. It is so final, so ultimate. Although death may win some earthly battles and have the temporary victory, we know Jesus will come again soon and will win the everlasting victory. Like the song, "Christ is Risen" by Matt Maher says, "Oh, death! Where is your sting? Oh hell! Where is your victory? Oh, Church! Come stand in the light! The glory of God has defeated the night!" Christ *is* risen from the grave, and He *has* trampled death by His death! I am so thankful that it's not the end of the story yet. To God be the glory!

We invite you to view the complete
selection of titles we publish at:

www.TEACHServices.com

Please write or email us your praises, reactions, or
thoughts about this or any other book we publish at:

TEACH Services, Inc.
P U B L I S H I N G
www.TEACHServices.com • (800) 367-1844

11 Quartermaster Circle
Fort Oglethorpe, GA 30742

info@TEACHServices.com

TEACH Services, Inc., titles may be purchased in bulk for
educational, business, fund-raising, or sales promotional use.
For information, please e-mail:

BulkSales@TEACHServices.com

Finally, if you are interested in seeing
your own book in print, please contact us at

publishing@TEACHServices.com

We would be happy to review your manuscript for free.

CPSIA information can be obtained
at www.ICGtesting.com
Printed in the USA
FFOW02n0009200916
27741FF